MODESTY

MODESTY

More Than a Change of Clothes

MARTHA PEACE & KENT KELLER

P&R PUBLISHING

P.O. BOX 817 • PHILLIPSBURG • NEW JERSEY 08865-0817

Unless otherwise indicated, Scripture is taken from the NEW AMERICAN STANDARD BIBLE®, Copyright ©1960, 1962, 1963, 1968, 1971, 1972, 1973, 1975, 1977 by the Lockman Foundation. Used by permission. All rights reserved. www.Lockman.org.

Scripture quotations marked (NIV) are from the HOLY BIBLE, NEW INTERNATIONAL VERSION®. NIV®. Copyright © 1973, 1978, 1984 by International Bible Society. Used by permission of Zondervan Publishing House. All rights reserved.

Scripture quotation from the Phillips New Testament in Modern English is taken from J. B. Phillips: The New Testament in Modern English, Revised Edition. Copyright © J. B. Phillips 1958, 1960, 1972. Used by permission of Macmillan Publishing Company.

Italics within Scripture quotations indicate emphasis added. Bracketed words within Scripture quotations indicate added explanations.

ISBN: 978-1-62995-081-5 (pbk)
ISBN: 978-1-62995-082-2 (ePub)
ISBN: 978-1-62995-083-9 (Mobi)

Printed in the United States of America

Library of Congress Control Number: 2015944779

This book is dedicated to my dear friend,
Marilyn Sherman, who lives in Anchorage, Alaska.
Her life is an amazing testimony of God's grace
as He has used her greatly in other people's lives for His glory!
—Martha

I would like to dedicate this book to my wife, Alana,
who is modest and beautiful inside and out,
and is my most precious gift on earth
next to salvation in Christ Jesus.
—Pastor Kent

Modesty: An inner attitude of the heart motivated by a love for God that seeks His glory through purity and humility; it often reveals itself in words, actions, expressions, and clothes.

Contents

Acknowledgments

Writing the acknowledgments is always my favorite part when it is time to publish any book I write. I want to thank the editorial team at P&R Publishing for their helpful and encouraging suggestions as we worked toward completing this project. Two others who helped are my husband, Sanford, and our daughter, Anna Maupin. They are always my biggest encouragers. Anna, on the one hand, is the one who makes all my books ultimately readable! Sanford, on the other hand, is my expert computer person. I do not know if he is really an expert, but compared to me, he definitely is!

And then there is Kent! Since he and I had never done anything like this together, we both went into it with a little bit of trepidation. However, at the end, I think that working with him was the best part of all. I have learned so much from him, and we had fun along the way. Kent had already completed the difficult part of research and writing. It was an honor for me to be able to tag on at the end. Thank you, Kent.

Now to Him who is able to do far more abundantly beyond all that we ask or think . . . to Him be the glory in the church and in Christ Jesus to all generations forever and ever. Amen. (Ephesians 3:20–21)

—Martha Peace

Many family and friends made significant contributions to my portion of this book. Thank you, Alana, for your many helpful suggestions, your continuous example of modesty, and your undying support! Kendal and Lauren, thank you for giving me the time to work on this book and much practical experience in working through the issues of modesty. My thanks also go to my parents, George and Doris Keller, who taught me to love the Bible from my earliest days.

There are also many godly men through the years who have taught me to love God and His Word. I am especially indebted to Dr. George Zemek, whose voice I hear in my mind when studying God's Word. Thank you for your friendship and the time you took to read through the manuscript and offer many valuable suggestions.

John, my pastor and friend, thank you for your help in reading through this manuscript and your suggestions for how to improve it. Anna, your editing was a gift from God as you helped me to learn what it means to write a book. Thanks also for having your English class of teens work through this and offer suggestions from their unique perspectives.

I'm also thankful for the staff at P&R. Thank you for improving this project in countless ways.

Martha, thanks for joining me in this project! Your experience and insights were a continual blessing from God for me. Without you, this book would have been dead in the water!

Ultimately, everything that is good is from God (James 1:17), and He deserves all praise for any good that might come from this book (Psalm 115:1)!

—KENT KELLER

PART ONE

Modesty Really *Is* More Than a Change of Clothes

A Word from Martha

The Lord saved me when I was thirty-three years old. At that time, I was a wife and a mother of an eleven-year-old daughter and a seven-year-old son. Before my salvation, I would have been characterized as a flirt who partied and drank too much. The Lord changed me a lot when he saved me. He gave me a new heart that desired to please Him above all else, but since I was a new Christian, there was a lot that I did not know. It took time for me to grow in my understanding of how to live the Christian life.

One area that I eventually became convicted of was the matter of the clothing styles of that day—*skintight jeans*. Not only did I wear them, but our daughter, Anna, wore them too. It was not difficult for me to give up wearing skintight jeans, but for Anna it was a different story. I explained why both of us had to change how we dressed, but she did not agree. Several times, we went shopping and both of us came home in tears with her vehemently hating every pair of jeans in the store that I thought were appropriate.

My husband, Sanford, and I talked about the problem, and he suggested that *he* would go shopping with us and *he* would make the final decision. One evening at supper, we explained to Anna that both her daddy and I were going to take her shopping the next morning, and that he would make the final decision about the jeans. Anna's little brother, David, was also at the supper table quietly listening to our conversation.

Anna was not pleased with the idea, burst into tears, got up from the table, and proceeded to walk out of the kitchen. Sanford and I were a little stunned at her reaction, but David was thrilled and called out to her as she headed toward the door: "Bye bye, Baggy Britches!"

It was quite the scene—Anna cried even louder, and Sanford and I doubled over laughing. We tried to contain ourselves, but absolutely could not. I doubt that Anna has yet forgiven David for that comment! It has been so many years that I do not remember exactly what happened the next day, but I think we did go shopping, and Anna abided by her daddy's wishes.

Fast-forward to the present and the issue of *skintight jeans* is almost nothing compared to the styles of today. The lower the cut of the blouse, the shorter the skirt, and, of course, the tighter the skinny jeans, the better. The challenges are greater and the styles even more immodest, but there is one thing that never changes:

> The LORD looks from heaven;
> He sees all the sons of men;
> From His dwelling place He looks out
> On all the inhabitants of the earth. (Psalm 33:13–14)

Before you read any further, stop and pray and ask the Lord this question: what does He see when He looks at you?

A Word from Pastor Kent

Picture with me a beautiful set of precious earrings: 24-karat gold, big, expensive, heavy—the perfect accessory for any outfit. You wouldn't want to wear these earrings doing outdoor activities because they are so valuable. These earrings would be reserved for special occasions.

Melt these two earrings into one earring, making it that much more precious. Now change the earring into a nose ring and put it in the nose of a sloppy, fat pig whose greatest delight is sticking its nose in the deepest part of the muddy puddle it calls home. When it's feeding time, the pig slurps up every last drop of hog slop it can find! Unfortunately, it has problems grabbing that last piece of food that has lodged itself in the nose ring. Finally, the food becomes rotten enough, and it falls off the nose ring. The pig squeals in happy delight just before licking up the tasty morsel! To make matters worse, while he is rooting around in his mud pit, the nose ring falls off. The continued trampling under the pig's feet plants the nose ring deep in the mud, never to see the light of day again. What a colossal waste!

OK, perhaps pigs aren't *that* sloppy, and farmers aren't that crazy to dress their pigs with gold nose rings. To be honest, this is quite an absurd picture. That is probably why Solomon used this picture to teach his children to be wise. In Proverbs 11:22 he writes, "As a ring of gold in a swine's snout, so is a beautiful woman who lacks discretion."

Solomon shows how shocking and inappropriate it is for a beautiful woman to act without discernment. One who "lacks discretion" is not able to make wise choices in life and can't discern what is right and what is wrong. When we're deciding what we should wear and how we should act, we need to exercise discernment. A beautiful woman who dresses and acts immodestly is uglier to God than a pig wearing a gold nose ring is to you.

This book was written to help you gain discernment in the area of modesty, because of the challenge it is to deal with the issue of immodesty. Modesty is more than just a change of clothes. It is an attitude of the heart. As a father of two girls, I deeply desire for my daughters to understand God's will for them regarding modesty in order that they might please Him in this area. As a youth pastor for many years, I found immodesty to be a growing, difficult issue to address with teens and their parents.

In Psalm 19:14, the psalmist humbly pleads,

> Let the words of my mouth and the meditation of my heart
> Be acceptable in Your sight,
> O LORD, my rock and my Redeemer.

What about you? What are your desires? Is God working in *your* heart? Is the prayer of the psalmist your prayer also?

Review Questions

1. According to Psalm 33:13–14, where is the LORD and what does He see?
2. Did you pray and ask God what He sees when He looks at you? If not, would you ask Him now?
3. Write out Proverbs 11:22.
4. What does it mean to "lack discretion"?
5. According to Psalm 19:14, what two areas in his life did the psalmist want to be acceptable to God?

1

What Is Immodesty, Anyway?

A Word from Martha

Have you ever heard the story of the frog that was placed in a pot full of cool water? The frog liked water and he was very happy. But then, very gradually, the heat was turned up under the bottom of the pan. So, gradually, the frog got used to the heat. After a while, the water was close to boiling, and the frog was in great danger, although he did not realize it.

Well, that is how clothing styles are today. Back in my great-grandmother Alice's day, in Victorian times, the women wore long dresses with high necks and bustles.

Thankfully fashions have changed, and I, for one, am glad! I bet you are, too! Clothing today is so much more comfortable and easy to care for than it used to be. The problem, though, is the extremes—the Victorian women covered up almost everything, but the fashions of our day cover up almost nothing! Like the frog in the water, we have gradually gotten used to the clothing styles of *our* day.

I am confident, though, that most of you want to figure out how to fit in with the styles of today. Certainly you do not want to look like Laura Ingalls Wilder in the *Little House on the Prairie* television series, much less like my great-grandmother Alice! Even though I am probably the age of most of your grandmothers, I don't want to look like either one of those either.

Frogs are stupid and they do not have a soul. Before they

know it, they are stuck in boiling water. We do not have to be like that. God has given us intelligence and created us in His image. Not only that, He can give us a new heart that loves Him and wants to please Him. We *can* glorify God in the way we dress, even while buying clothes in our day and age.

Modesty is shown by how we dress, but it is a much bigger issue than just our outward clothing. In the next section, Pastor Kent is going to tell you why.

A Word from Pastor Kent

In some Christian circles, it is considered immodest for adults to wear shorts of any kind. Other well-meaning Christians provide measurements, like saying that shorts and skirts should be no shorter than three inches above the knee when a person is seated. At the beach or a swimming pool, which swimsuits are modest and which are immodest?

Other cultures define the standard of modesty differently. For example, Islamic cultures often require that women wear a *hijab* or a *burkha* that covers a woman from head to toe with only the hands and skin around the eyes showing. The purpose for this is to prevent immodesty and lust, but is a hijab the best solution? While it is a sin to make others stumble by wearing too little clothing, is being covered from head to toe the answer? Figuring out exactly what it looks like to be modest or immodest can be difficult.

By now you may be asking, "When do my clothes cross the line into being 'out-of-bounds'? When is an outfit considered sinful?" But these aren't the best questions to ask. When your desire is to please God, you won't be interested in getting as close to the line of sin as possible without crossing over that line. Instead, you will want to stay as far away from this line of sin as is wise! Therefore, a better question should be, "What does God say it means to be modest and immodest, so that I will know how to please Him?"

What Is the Biblical Standard of Modesty?

A picture book would have been quite handy, but God chose in His infinitely perfect wisdom to give us words to answer this question. After all, the Scriptures were written "for our instruction" (Romans 15:4). The Bible tells us what we are doing wrong, teaches us how to correct it, *and* trains us to be godly (see 2 Timothy 3:16).

Based upon the Bible as revealed in the chapters that follow, this is our definition of modesty:

> Modesty is an inner attitude of the heart motivated by a love for God that seeks His glory through purity and humility; it often reveals itself in words, actions, expressions, and clothes.

If you have a heart[1] that loves God, you will want to please God. According to the Bible, the heart is the part of you that thinks your thoughts, makes the choices of your will, feels your emotions, and lives on after your death.

A heart that is concerned about pleasing God will express itself modestly by what you think, say, do, and wear. True modesty can come only from someone who is more concerned about showing the world how great God is than how great she is. True modesty doesn't come from changing one's wardrobe. It comes from having one's heart changed. If you want to be modest, your heart must follow after God. When you choose to be immodest (or commit any sin), then you are choosing your own sinful desires over God's desires, showing that He is not first in your life—at least not at that moment.

God can again be first in your heart when you repent from your sin and believe in His Son Jesus Christ (Mark 1:15). Repenting from sin means that you change your view of sin so that you live as God desires. What used to seem fun or desirable is now seen as something that God hates, so you want to turn from that sin. God is first in your heart when you believe that Jesus is the only one who can save you from your sin. He is the Lord and Master of your heart. When He is most important to you, you want to please Him by doing what He commands, because you love Him! When God is first in your heart, you *will* be modest!

On the other hand,

> Immodesty is an attitude of the heart that expresses itself with inappropriate words, actions, expressions and/or clothes that are flirtatious, manipulative, revealing, or suggestive of sensuality or pride.

Just as with modesty, the immodesty we can see comes from an immodest heart, which we can't see. You can, however, measure the heart by the fruit that your life produces (Matthew 7:20). If you want to act or dress immodestly so that you catch the attention of all the guys, or at least that cute one who you wish would pay more attention to you, God is not first in your heart.

If you haven't found out already, some guys can be manipulated pretty easily. This desire to get them to do what you want by flirting, behaving, or dressing immodestly does not honor God. This does not come from a pure heart, but from a sinful desire for attention that dishonors God.

A Diagnosis of Immodesty

Just as doctors are able to diagnose diseases by looking at a person's symptoms, sinful immodesty can be diagnosed by various symptoms.

If you find yourself making some of the following symptomatic statements, you may be dressing immodestly. This isn't always the case, but each of these statements finds its source in a lack of knowledge about Scripture, at best, or a rebellious heart, at worst. If you simply have never seen these things from the Bible's point of view, then this book should help you make some changes that might even be easy for you to make. So, have you ever said or thought any of the following? (Be honest with yourself if you want an accurate diagnosis of your heart.)

- "I *do* dress modestly compared to *most* girls. Since I'm more modest than most, I must be dressing modestly."
- "I don't want to dress like my grandma! No one will want to hang around with someone dressed in some 'old-fashioned' way. I want to dress fashionably, *not* frumpily." (OK, you may not say "frumpily," but you get the picture.)
- "Some guy's problem with lust is not *my* problem. Quit blaming me for his problems. We already have too much of that 'victim' mentality that wants to pass the blame to others in our culture today."
- "If I dress modestly, then that guy will just lust after someone else. What difference does it make?"
- "I *want* to get that guy's attention. I'm tired of sitting home on Friday nights all by myself. I like the attention I get when I show off a bit."
- "This is all just legalism. I can dress any way I want to since this is a 'gray area.'"
- "My mother does not have a clue about how to dress!"
- "Who *cares* what the Bible says! I'll dress like I want!"

These statements do not by any means represent all that it means to be immodest, but if you find yourself thinking these thoughts, you need to understand and follow what the Bible says about modesty.

Has anyone ever come to you, out of love and care for you, and pointed out that you may be immodest? How did you respond? Did you listen to what that person said and ask God to evaluate your heart? Proverbs is clear that those who are wise listen to the rebuke of others, while fools don't. For example, Proverbs 12:15 tells us, "The way of a fool is right in his own eyes, but a wise man is he who listens to counsel" (see also Proverbs 15:31; 19:20).

Maybe the person rebuking you for immodesty was wrong. She may have been inappropriately legalistic in her understanding of Scripture. But did you at least consider what she had to say?

As you read more, you will understand what is at stake and what the Bible says about the need for modesty. Before we dive into what the Bible teaches about modesty, though, I believe it would be helpful for you to understand what makes guys so different, especially in the way they think.

Review Questions

1. Fill in the blanks from the definition of modesty in this chapter. "An inner _____ of _____ motivated by _____ for God that seeks His _____ through _____ and _____ that often reveals itself in words, actions, expressions, and clothes."
2. Restate the definition of immodesty in your own words.
3. What does the Bible mean when it talks about your heart?
4. What does it mean to "repent from sin"?
5. According to Proverbs 15:31 and 19:20, what should you think if someone tells you that you dress immodestly?
6. If you really think that person is wrong (and it may well be the case), then what should you do?

2

How Are Guys So Different?

A Word from Martha

Can you think of someone who was cruel to you? Perhaps another kid at school made fun of you in front of others, and everyone laughed. Perhaps he pushed you or tried to trip you up. Maybe he grabbed your books, ran down the hall with them, and threw them in a trashcan. As a result, you dreaded going to school because that bully of a kid would not leave you alone.

You tried everything you could think of to stop him—yelling back in anger, telling the teacher, telling your parents, crying, and begging him to stop. One day you even tried praying for him. On the days when The Bully did not make fun of you, you were nonetheless well aware that he was lurking near you, ready to burst forth with seemingly endless cruelty at any moment. You *always* had to be on guard and try, very hard, to avoid him.

In a similar way, that is how boys usually are when they see an immodestly dressed woman. Even if they try to be godly, they are well aware of the sexual temptation. Think about it: you can be perfectly happy at school, talking and laughing with your friends, and then you see The Bully coming straight at you. Panic and despair immediately grip your heart. You have an instantaneous emotional reaction. Then you have a physical reaction—your heart rate increases, your cheeks turn red, and perhaps tears well up in your eyes.

Well, typically when men see an immodestly dressed woman,

they have an instantaneous physical reaction: sexual temptation. It can happen to them out of the blue. It is like someone hit them "upside the head" with a baseball bat that they didn't see coming. It is just as difficult, if not more difficult, for men to avoid sexual temptation as it is for you to avoid reacting to The Bully.

Since "our ambition . . . [is] to be pleasing to Him" (2 Corinthians 5:9), let's analyze this situation biblically. We will begin with the big, overall picture.

The Two Greatest Commands

The Pharisees, the religious leaders of Jesus' day, were jealous of the Lord, and they were often trying to trick Him into doing or saying something wrong. They believed that doing good works and staying away from anything or anyone who, in their thinking, was unclean made you acceptable to God. They were so zealous in their pursuit that they made up additional rules that were not in the Scriptures. In fact, they made up hundreds of them! That was called the Talmud, and the Pharisees believed that their Talmud-rules were almost as important as the Scriptures.

If making up their own rules in order to be holy was not strange enough, the Pharisees also divided God's Law (including their Talmud) into what they determined to be the "greater laws" and the "lesser laws." The "greater laws" were what they believed they needed to keep, and the "lesser laws" were *optional*. How convenient for them!

So it was not illogical, in their way of thinking, to ask Jesus which one He thought was the greatest law. They got a really smart man, who was trained to interrogate people, to ask the question. Jesus answered, "'You shall *love the Lord your God* with all your heart, and with all your soul, and with all your mind.' This is the great and foremost commandment" (Matthew 22:37–38).

It is interesting, though, that Jesus did not stop there. He added the second most important commandment and explained that it was similar to the first one. "The second is like it, 'You shall *love your neighbor* as yourself'" (Matthew 22:39). The Pharisees had lost sight of what it *meant* to love God with all your heart. The Lord Jesus made it clear when He told us *how* to show our love to God: "If you love Me, you will keep My commandments" (John 14:15).

So, what does this mean for us? Particularly regarding the topic of immodesty? Plainly put, we should not dress or act in any way that would cause another person to be tempted to sin. The Bible tells us we are not to be a "stumbling block to the weak" (1 Corinthians 8:9). Since men are weaker in this area, we females should try to make it as easy as possible for them to remain pure. Because we should love God, we should *desire* to please Him in these ways.

Think about 1 Corinthians 13:4–7.

> Love is patient, love is kind, *and* is not jealous; love does not brag *and* is not arrogant, does not act unbecomingly; it does not seek its own, is not provoked, does not take into account a wrong *suffered*, does not rejoice in unrighteousness, but rejoices with the truth; bears all things, believes all things, hopes all things, endures all things.

This is the famous passage that describes how love behaves. One of the facets of love shows us that it "does not rejoice in unrighteousness, but rejoices with the truth" (1 Corinthians 13:6). A woman could show love to the men in her life, whether she personally knows them or not, by not dressing in a way that would entice them to think of her in an unrighteous manner.

Now that you know The Bully of sexual temptation that men undergo due to what they see and feel, I want you to think about this and analyze it in two ways: Am I showing love to God? And am I showing love to others?

A Word from Pastor Kent

Besides some obvious physical differences, God has designed guys to think and respond differently than girls do. There are many ways this shows itself. One example is that, when an attractive woman walks into a room, guys are typically tempted to lust after *her*, while women are typically tempted to act like it is a secret beauty pageant and envy her appearance or lust after the *attention* she is getting. So, in the same situation, guys and girls tend to respond completely differently.

Usually guys are more drawn by what they see in real life or in pictures, while women are more drawn by emotional relationships. That's why 40 percent of all paperback book sales are romance novels.[1] Just in case you were wondering, guys are not the ones buying all those! If you keep that distinction in mind—typically, women daydream about romance and men daydream about sex—you'll be well on your way to understanding how different men are, at least in how they respond to what they see.

The Biblical View of the Sin of Lust

The original word for lust, as it is used in the New Testament, really only means "a strong desire." Normally, though, this word is used to refer to sinful desires and often sinful sexual desires. These sinful desires can be wanting something that God has said is not good for us or wanting something that *is* good for us but in ways that are not healthy. For example, God created food to be good for us. But if I eat only chocolate cookies all day long, so much so that I even become sick from this unhealthy diet, a good desire for food has been twisted into a sinful desire that makes me sick.

Lust is always dangerous! This is how the apostle John explained it.

> Do not love the world nor the things in the world. If anyone loves the world, the love of the Father is not in him. For all that is in the world, the lust of the flesh and the lust of the eyes and the boastful pride of life, is not from the Father, but is from the world. The world is passing away, and also its lusts; but the one who does the will of God abides forever. (1 John 2:15–17)

Obviously lust is not unique to men only. Both men and women struggle with sinful desires.

The Man's Struggle

As I write about men's struggle with lust, remember that I'm talking about men *generally*. Not all men wrestle with sexual lust to the same extent. As you interact with specific guys in your life, remember that only God knows what they are thinking. You are called not to be a mind reader or judge, but rather to give others the benefit of the doubt (see 1 Corinthians 13:7). This doesn't mean that you should be naive—pay attention and act wisely, especially when you feel uncomfortable—but be careful not to focus on what someone *might* be thinking.

When a woman learns how common an issue sexual lust is for men, she can be tempted to think the worst of them. In contrast, when a man learns this, he can be tempted to rationalize his sinful, lustful thoughts as being normal and acceptable. In other words, he might think that it's no big deal because it seems that every other guy has the same struggle. It is *not* a sin to be tempted or to feel attracted to someone. It is sin, though, to linger on that attraction and allow yourself to desire what God says is not good for you. Guys have supernatural power through Christ to renew their minds and not be affected by immodesty.

The sinful, natural response to immodesty, though, is lust. Jesus warned men about sexual lust in the heart when He said,

> You have heard that it was said, "You shall not commit adultery"; but I say to you that everyone who looks on a woman with lust for her has already committed adultery with her in his heart. (Matthew 5:27–28)

Your heart is simply who you are on the inside, the realm of your thoughts, feelings, and decisions. Only God truly knows what is in your heart (Jeremiah 17:9–10).

Job understood this principle before Jesus taught this. He said he had made a covenant with his eyes to avoid temptations to lust (Job 31:1). A covenant is an agreement between two parties. Job's covenant was between himself and God. Because Job loved God, he decided *not* to allow his eyes to linger but to immediately turn his eyes and mind away from lust.

Guys do have problems with sinful lust. But men are not the only ones with this problem. Women do too, and they have ways of luring guys.

How Women Fish

It seems like fishing is more of a guy thing than something for girls. This is true, however, only with those slimy swimming things called fish. Girls do a lot of fishing as well—for those cute walking things called guys. One obvious way that girls fish is by the way they dress.

Unfortunately, guys don't typically respond to a girl's fishing techniques the way she wants them to respond. She may simply be trying to catch some cute guy's attention, but she may end up catching the *lustful* attention of a guy who sees her immodesty as an invitation to think sexually about her and possibly act sexually toward her. Remember, sinful lust's only desire is to gratify itself. It does not care about God or about anyone else.

The following conversation between a Christian author and the father of a college-aged daughter vividly reveals what can be going on in a guy's heart.

> One father asked me why his normally cautious college-aged daughter dressed in a tight little top and skirt around a particular guy she found attractive. "Surely," this father said, "surely she knows what she's doing!"
>
> "Yes," I agreed, "she knows she looks good. But she doesn't realize what is actually going on in that guy's head. What she's smugly thinking is, *He thinks I'm cute.*"
>
> "Cute has nothing to do with it!" the shocked father replied. "He's picturing her *naked!*"[2]

Not only is it a little confusing to understand what kind of "fish" you are catching with the lure of immodesty, but it is also important to understand how quickly immodesty works. A guy needs little time for his desires to develop. And if he allows this to happen, the temptation can be all-consuming. It can almost feel like a blow to the stomach in its sudden domination of the heart.

I've noticed that guys have a hard time focusing on what they are saying when they are tempted to lust after a woman. If a guy is unprepared mentally to respond biblically to lust, his mouth goes on autopilot the second that temptation walks by, and he spouts useless words or just stops mid-sentence while lust consumes the mind. The conversation is no longer fluid but halts until he remembers that he was talking before he allowed himself to be interrupted. Some guys can cover their lustful thoughts better than others can, but it normally takes practice to master such levels of hypocrisy.

In order for a guy to satisfy his lust, he may act how you want him to act for a while, but you should understand that he has a different goal in mind. Once his lust is aroused, he may act in ways that you don't like. You may be fishing for a colorful rainbow trout, but you may catch a great white shark!

Is It Really That Difficult for Guys?

Girls, it is important for you to understand that this struggle is very difficult for guys. Part of the problem could be that you don't truly comprehend the man's struggle. When John Crotts, the pastor-teacher of the church I attend, preached on modesty, he used the illustration of an iceberg. You can see only about 10 percent of an iceberg, and the rest is removed from sight. This illustrates the effect of lust upon the typical guy who doesn't resist this temptation to sin. You can see only a small fraction of what is going on in his heart. When his lusts are inflamed, he'll give you what you want in order to get what he wants! So don't manipulate or be manipulated! The attention that comes from sinful lust is never, ever satisfying. It is not one of love, gentleness, and care. It can, however, look like that satisfying type of attention—at least for a while, on the surface.

Another vivid picture of how difficult it is for a man not to lust after an immodestly dressed woman comes to us from one of the sermons of a seventeenth-century pastor, Richard Baxter.[3] This part of the sermon was to help women understand the man's struggle. Baxter suggested that you think of yourself as a candle in a room that is filled with gunpowder. Gunpowder is harmless until it is exposed to a flame. When exposed to a flame, it immediately blows the entire building to bits. You cannot take it back once the explosion happens. Therefore, protect your flame (be modest) so that you do not ignite explosive, sinful passion in guys who are quickly and easily inflamed by immodesty.

I may seem a little old-fashioned, somewhat out of touch with the here and now. Perhaps I sound a little bit like your dad—but, like your dad and like God, I want you to have a blessed life and, if the Lord wills, to marry the godly "man of your dreams." So, I do want to tell you about . . .

The Godly Perspective of Modesty in Marriage

There is one context in which a woman can reveal and even celebrate her beauty in full. I believe God made a man to be visually stimulated to enjoy the beauty of his wife in the God-designed context called marriage!

When God made Eve and presented her to Adam, Adam's words conveyed a sense of excitement upon seeing her. The translation, "This is now bone of my bones, and flesh of my flesh," doesn't really carry out this idea very well. One of my seminary professors translated these words from Genesis 2:23 to say, "*Wow!*"

After looking at and naming all the animals all day long, Adam must have been absolutely stunned by this gorgeous, perfectly made, God-designed woman who was to be his wife. Maybe Adam was so stunned that all he could come up with was "This is now bone of *my* bones, and flesh of *my* flesh." He may have reverted back to giving her a name (2:23) simply because he was too overwhelmed for any romantic lines, especially since he had no prior romantic experience. Being visually stimulated is God's design for men as a gift to be enjoyed in the context of marriage!

Solomon pictures this enjoyment in Proverbs 5:19. A husband is to be satisfied with and intoxicated in his physical relationship with his wife. You are to enjoy the sensual nature of the physical relationship in marriage. A wife is to show off the beauty of her form to her husband in the context of marriage as God's delightful gift to him, and the husband likewise gives his body to his wife for her enjoyment (1 Corinthians 7:3–4).

Until marriage, the charms of your physical beauty and femininity need to be wrapped carefully in modesty so that you will have the gift of purity to give to your husband once you are married. For now and in the future, whether you marry or not, guard your heart from those romantic thoughts and feelings that create discontent and a desire for things that do not please the Lord.

What is your heart's desire? Is it to be pure before the Lord and to help the men (who are everywhere!) not to struggle with sinful lust when they see you? Take some time now and ask the Lord to help you be the godly woman that He wants you to become.

Review Questions

1. What are the two greatest commands? Where are they found in the Bible?

2. In John 14:15, how did Jesus say we can show love to God?

3. According to 1 Corinthians 8:9; 1 Timothy 2:9; and 1 Corinthians 13:6, why should we not dress or act in a way that would tempt guys to lust in their hearts?

4. Explain the difference between acceptable desires and sinful desires.

5. Pastor Kent wrote about a "fishing" illustration. How does he describe some guys' reactions to seeing an immodest woman? How long does it take for them to react?

6. What is the one circumstance in which a woman can fully reveal her beauty to another?

7. How did Adam react when he saw Eve for the first time?

PART TWO

The Old Testament on Immodesty

A Word from Martha and Pastor Kent

Today, many Christians focus exclusively upon the New Testament to find guidance for how we should live. If the Old Testament is studied, quite often it is only for those exciting stories that show God's amazing power. But three-fourths of what God has revealed in His Word is found in the Old Testament.

If we ignore this vast reservoir of revelation in the Old Testament, we miss out on much that is important for guiding how we should live. Any accurate understanding of the New Testament will ultimately be based on what God has given in the Old Testament. That is why Paul told Timothy that "All Scripture is inspired by God and profitable" (2 Timothy 3:16), referring primarily to the Old Testament.[1]

If we ignore what God revealed in the Old Testament regarding immodesty, in particular, we will miss out on a wealth of material that helps us to understand God's view of this issue. Let's see what God has to teach us about immodesty from the Old Testament.

3

Why Should I Wear Clothes?

A Word from Martha

Recently, my husband and I were eating in a local restaurant and a teenage girl walked in. *Almost everyone* noticed her because she was so scantily clad—much worse than the typical immodest styles of today. I was a little shocked at how she was dressed, and I thought, "My goodness, she is practically naked!" Then her mother walked in, and *everyone* noticed her because they, like me, thought, "She *is* naked!"

Well, of course, she was not completely naked, but she may as well have been. Both mother and daughter should have been embarrassed, but they were not. Their suggestive and immodest clothing was, as the expression goes, "over the top!" As I thought about it, I realized, "How sad for that young woman that her mother set such a blatantly sensual example by tempting the men in that restaurant." A more old-timey word for how they should have felt would be *shame*.

"Shame, Shame on You!"

Years ago, when children misbehaved, it was common to hear their mothers say, "You naughty child, *shame on you!*" Nowadays, mothers don't play the "shame on you" card or call their children "naughty." They probably do not want their children to feel bad about themselves. But is this really the best way to think about sin and guilt?

No, the Scriptures teach us that sin is real and that we are guilty and should feel ashamed when we violate God's standards. Even if our mothers do not instruct us concerning the right way to dress, we are still responsible before God to do what is right. There simply are some things that we *should* feel guilty about. Immodesty is one of those things.

There is something interesting about sinful desires. They can never, ever be satisfied, no matter how immodestly you dress or how flirtatious you act. All of that attention from others is, perhaps, exciting for the moment, but the next moment you will find that you crave more and more. This reminds me of the following Proverb: "The leech has two daughters: [their names are] 'Give,' [and] 'Give'" (Proverbs 30:15). The first time I read that proverb, it made me laugh; but, actually, it is so true. We want more and more and more. That is why someone can be drawn further and further into sin until everyone around her is thinking, "How could she *possibly* go out in public dressed like that?"

There are a couple of answers to that question. One is that the person caught up in any sin may not really know the Lord. The second answer is that her conscience has likely been seared. After sinning long enough, she does not feel guilt at all. (Remember the frog in water that slowly heated up?) So, either way, she cannot be sensitive to what God tells us is right, good, and pure.

Could that ever change? Is there any hope? Of course! God *can* work in people's lives to show them their sin, cleanse them from sin, and grant them faith in Christ and repentance. Repentance is a grace gift from God. Repentance is turning from sin and turning to Jesus Christ to want to please Him. People who do this have the Holy Spirit indwelling them to convict them concerning what *sin* is and what *righteousness* is.

In summary, the first answer to why sin is never satisfied is that the people sinning do not know the Lord. They are spiritually lost in their "trespasses and sins" (Ephesians 2:1) and need God's enabling grace to help them repent. The second answer to why these people's sin is never satisfied is that their conscience has been seared. I am going to let Pastor Kent explain this to you.

A Word from Pastor Kent

Someone, probably in all sincerity, will think that the origin of clothes is "The store, of course." This chapter is not designed to point out where you could, or should, buy your clothes. Rather, it is concerned with the origin of clothes so that we will understand why appropriate clothing is so important.

If snow is a regular part of your winter weather, you certainly understand one reason why clothes are important! The reason for wearing clothes, however, is much more significant than just keeping you warm. Clothes are not primarily about fashion, style, trying to fit in with your friends, or even warmth. The God-given reason for wearing clothes is to *cover our nakedness* so that we do not experience *guilt and shame for sin*. It is embarrassing to be found naked! The reason for this goes all the way back to the earliest history of mankind and was given during the beginning of our universe in Genesis 1–3.

Before Adam and Eve sinned in the garden, no clothes were needed. At the end of the sixth day of creation, when everything had been created, it was all "very good" (Genesis 1:31). Creation was perfect, exactly the way God wanted to be! Moses writes that, after the creation of man and woman on the sixth day, "the man and his wife were both naked and were not ashamed" (Genesis 2:25). Why should they be ashamed? They were husband and wife (2:24), no one else existed on earth, and there was no sin! Under these conditions, nakedness was God's design, and there was no possibility for shame. Clothes simply were not needed. (It must have been warm in the garden of Eden!)

Seven verses later (Genesis 3:7), Adam and Eve *were* ashamed of their nakedness and made clothes for themselves. They were still married and no other humans existed yet. *What happened?* Sin happened. The only difference between shame*less* nakedness and shame*ful* nakedness was that they were now sinners.

Satan tempted Eve to doubt God (3:1), and the rest is history—our history. After Adam and Eve ate from the Tree of Knowledge of Good and Evil, "Then the eyes of both of them were opened, and they knew that they were naked; and they sewed fig leaves together and made themselves loin coverings" (Genesis 3:7).[1]

Man's Faulty Attempt

Adam and Eve tried their own solution and covered their "loins" with fig leaves. The Hebrew word for "loin covering" in Genesis 3:7 refers to a "belt" in the rest of Scripture.[2] This article, when worn by women, "was not an undergarment . . . but a valuable ornamental belt or sash"[3] (see Proverbs 31:24; Isaiah 3:24). When men wore this article of clothing, they hung their sword from it (1 Samuel 18:4).[4] This word is used to describe something that was much too immodest to cover nakedness.

The fig leaf garment that Adam and Eve made was obviously a quickly designed, inadequate covering for their nakedness. Derek Kidner puts it this way: "The *fig leaves* were pathetic enough, as human . . . [attempts] tend to be, but the instinct was sound and God confirmed it, for sin's proper fruit is shame."[5]

Adam and Eve had the right idea; clothes were now needed to cover their nakedness. They did not choose the right kind of clothing, though, so God corrected their faulty attempt.

God's Solution

The word for "garments" (Genesis 3:21), which God made for Adam and Eve to cover their nakedness, is also translated as "tunic."[6] A tunic was a long shirt that reached down to the knees or ankles.

Since Genesis doesn't come with divinely inspired pictures, we don't know exactly what the garments that God made for Adam and Eve looked like. It is safe to assume that what God made covered a whole lot more skin than what Adam and Eve made. These garments covered their nakedness, which in turn covered their shame. Therefore, their very clothing was a reminder that they had sinned against God and could no longer be innocent in the presence of God or each other.

Clothes Remind Us of Our Sin

Why do some people dress immodestly? What is the heart motive behind what they do? In other words, what are they thinking and desiring? Immodest dress may be a sign that some are trying to reject the idea of sin itself, since clothes are meant to cover us from the shame of sin. And, if there is no sin, then they may each think, "I am not a sinner who will be judged by God!"

Others do know what God's Word says, but don't care. In other words, they have no fear of God. Scripture says that they are actively suppressing God's truth (Romans 1:18–21). Rather than honoring God, they reject His Word and sear their conscience (1 Timothy 4:2). They may feel some guilt or self-consciousness at first, but the longer the sin goes on, the less guilt they feel. The seared conscience is then silent, allowing the silence to be confused with the feeling of "I am doing nothing wrong."

Shame due to "nakedness" was paid for by death, the death of Jesus Christ. The apostle Peter reminds Christians that they were redeemed "with precious blood, as of a lamb unblemished and spotless, the blood of Christ" (1 Peter 1:19). Today, any sin (including immodesty) can be forgiven only through the death of Jesus. This sin is that serious!

The original purpose for clothing came about because people were no longer innocent but filled with sin. Even believers, who have been saved from slavery to sin, still experience the seduction of sin. Therefore, immodesty and sinful people make for an explosive combination. With this mixture, sin detonates to various degrees of destruction. God in His perfect wisdom provided clothing to prevent the destructive nature of sin. Remember that God, in His kindness, covered Adam and Eve's shame; and the Lord Jesus, in *His* kindness, has covered your shame if you are a Christian.

Keep in mind that there is a difference between the shame due to sin and being ashamed of how God made you. We should not feel shame about what we look like. The psalmist rejoices that he is "fearfully and wonderfully made" (Psalm 139:14). Remember to be thankful for how God has uniquely made you!

Review Questions

1. According to Martha's explanation, what is repentance? Where does it come from?
2. What is the God-given reason for wearing clothes?
3. Adam and Eve inadequately tried to cover themselves with fig leaves. What, then, did God do?
4. What happens when someone "sears her conscience"?
5. What are some of the possible motives for immodesty?

4

Why Were Women Immodest in the Old Testament?

A Word from Martha

In some ways, it's easier being a girl than a boy. We can fix our hair and makeup to enhance our natural beauty. We can play up our best features and cover up the ones we like less. We also have more options for clothing than the guys have. That is the good news. The bad news, though, is that we can use those freedoms in a sexually provocative way that results in sin against God and the men in our life.

You see, we are not really so different from the women in the Old Testament. Some of them were godly, and their outward beauty reflected a chaste, pure heart; some of them were prideful, and their outward beauty reflected vanity, sensuality, and immodesty.

Let's look at two of the godly women in the Old Testament. Certainly we do not have pictures of how they were dressed, but we do have some insight into their hearts.

The Excellent Wife (Proverbs 31:10–31)

This woman must have been something else! She is described as having worth "far above jewels" (Proverbs 31:10). She sews, she makes her own cloth on a loom, and she makes sure everyone in her household is clothed well. But what about her? How does she dress? We don't exactly know, but the Scriptures describe, in a rather picturesque way, how she dresses and clothes herself.

> She girds [dresses] herself with strength,
> And makes her arms strong. (Proverbs 31:17)

> Strength and dignity are her clothing,
> And she smiles at the future. (Proverbs 31:25)

We know from Proverbs that "the excellent wife" is not lazy and that she works hard. Thus, her arms are strong. We also know that she is calm and dignified and is not afraid of the future. In fact, I think she is looking forward to the future and what God is going to do. There are several other descriptions of this remarkable woman, but the most telling one of all is that she "fears the LORD" (Proverbs 31:30). That is her heart.

Sarah, a Holy Woman Who Hoped in God

Sarah was Abraham's wife. She lived an amazing life full of adventure and travel, and she saw some of God's promises to her husband fulfilled in supernatural ways. One of those promises was that Abraham would father a son in his old age. Sarah, too, was old! God made a covenant with Abraham and told him that he would be a father to multitudes and that the Messiah would come from his lineage.

Certainly, there are things that Sarah did wrong in her marriage to Abraham. But we know that, as a general pattern in her life, she *did* believe God and *was* a biblically submissive wife to Abraham. We know that because the apostle Peter describes her as a holy woman "who hoped in God" (1 Peter 3:5). We also know from the Old Testament that Sarah was a physically beautiful woman, but Peter highlights her true beauty.

For in this way in former times the holy women also, *who hoped in God, used to adorn themselves*, being submissive to their own husbands. Thus Sarah obeyed Abraham, calling him lord, and you have become her children if you do what is right without being frightened by any fear. (1 Peter 3:5–6)

Sarah was beautiful outwardly *and* inwardly. We could describe it as her "heart's beauty." Ultimately, she believed God and is described as a holy woman "who hoped in God." Her adornment was her godly submission to her husband and her hope in God. This was the overall pattern of her life. I remember, as a new Christian, reading 1 Peter. When I read about Sarah, I remember asking God to make me like one of "the holy women who hoped in God." Maybe you'd like to stop and pray and ask God for that, too?

A Word from Pastor Kent

In some ways, it's easier being a guy. When guys choose what clothes to wear, it seems like they choose clothes for one of two reasons: comfort, or a desire to impress someone—often a girl! For those who don't really care about how they look, comfort is the overriding motive in choosing clothes. Often, especially when some girl catches his eye, a guy like this will start caring more about how he looks. While it is possible for guys to dress immodestly (Speedo swimsuits and baggy pants falling down), there is seldom the same pressure for guys to dress that way.

It seems a little more complicated for women. First, most girls care about how they look. Second, as they get older and try to impress, there are more options for the kinds of clothing they may wear. Guys wear either shorts or pants. Women can wear shorts, pants, capris, skirts, skorts, leggings, or dresses. Compare how much more space in the average department store is devoted to women's clothing versus guys' clothing.

The more choices people have, the more complicated choosing becomes. Then this becomes even more complicated due to the motives behind those choices. We should ask God to reveal our own motives to us so that we might repent of those that are sinful. This will help us to glorify God by being modest.

First, we will look at *the* godly motive that pleases our great God—*fearing Him!* Then, second, we will look at two passages that reveal sinful motives for immodesty that are still quite common today, more than 2,500 years after they were written!

The Godly Motive behind Modesty

> Charm is deceitful and beauty is vain,
> But a woman who fears the LORD, she shall be praised.
> (Proverbs 31:30)

Ever read Proverbs 31? If not, take a minute to read it. It's an example of the kind of woman that God wants you to be! King Lemuel must have listened well when his wise mother taught him about feminine beauty. These are gifts of God to be used and enjoyed in ways that delight Him! So, be thankful for the charm and beauty that God has given to you! Nevertheless, Lemuel's mother describes so much more than just outward beauty.

This written portrait of an amazing woman concludes with the passage above and reveals a lie of our culture. This lie tells you that being beautiful is the key to a life of utter happiness and complete satisfaction. But if charm and beauty were the keys to satisfaction, our culture's constant pursuit of these traits would have long ago brought about utopia, utter perfection! And we know that hasn't happened.

The key to understanding this helpful verse is to see what is being contrasted with charm and beauty. Ancient Hebrew poetry was not based upon rhyming words as our poetry is today. For example, we probably would have written Proverbs 31:30 this way:

> Charm is deceitful and beauty is vain,
> But a woman will be praised when by the Lord she is trained.

The most important element in interpreting ancient Hebrew poetry correctly, though, is to understand how parallelism was used. The significance of parallelism in poetry is that the correct interpretation of a passage is found by studying the relationship between two or more lines that belong together. So what is the intent of Proverbs 31:30?

This verse teaches the contrast between the false appearance of satisfaction (charm and beauty) and that which truly satisfies (fearing God). Charm is deceitful in that it promises satisfaction but never truly delivers. Beauty is vain, or meaningless, when it comes to gratifying the desires of the soul. The beautiful charmer might get temporary applause, but what happens when the beauty fades or someone more beautiful wanders by? Any attention she draws is temporary and will fade as her external beauty and charm diminish.

Instead, true satisfaction comes from having a right relationship with God in which you draw close to Him in the fear of God. This fear certainly includes respect and reverence, but it means more than this. It means that you are afraid of displeasing Him, which causes you to grow in your relationship with Him. It isn't the kind of fear that makes you want to run and hide from Him. This fear of God brings us closer to Him. Our relationship with God will then bring profound and significant praise that lasts for eternity!

If your primary motive in life is to be charming and beautiful, then you are deceiving yourself with a vain, empty, or useless life purpose that will ultimately let you down because it leads you away from God. If your motive is to please God, you will find joy that is utterly satisfying as you depend upon Him for His grace and do what He says. The contrast is simple. Is the primary motive behind your appearance to please God or to please yourself? Do you want to be charming and beautiful for God's glory in order to draw attention to Him, or for your *own* glory in order to draw attention to *yourself*?

Modesty shows that you are someone under the authority of God, someone who fears Him. Rather than showing that you disbelieve God by focusing on charm and beauty, you choose to demonstrate your belief in God by being modest. We, as Christians, are to be good stewards of what God has entrusted to us, and that includes beauty and charm. It is God-glorifying to pursue beauty and charm as long as your motive is right and the result is to point others to God. For example, it can take a long time to find modest clothing in today's stores. But taking the time to find modest clothing, and sometimes spending more money for it, is a godly way of pursuing beauty for His glory.

The alternative is to make an idol out of beauty and charm. Imagine that, while walking to join your friends in the school cafeteria, you trip and manage to splash spaghetti sauce all over your new white shirt on the very day that school pictures are being taken. Does it crush your sense of beauty and destroy your mood? Responding in sinful ways (by complaining, getting angry, having a sour mood, or skipping class because you are hiding out in the girls' bathroom crying your heart out) shows that you have made an idol out of beauty and charm.

When you are focused upon yourself, you are not fearing God, at least at that moment. Sure, it's embarrassing as your pride takes a hit, but that's not all bad. It is good for our pride to be humbled. If you can laugh at yourself and your spaghetti-splattered outfit, this shows that you aren't taking yourself too seriously—which is good, because you are "not to think more highly of . . . [yourself] than . . . [you] ought to think" (Romans 12:3). If you respond to these kinds of challenges without sin, then you are living in the fear of God. Your fear of God will honor Him, as well as cause others to marvel at your response. Some might even ask you how you respond so well in difficult times. This is a way that people praise you for your fear of God, and it gives you an opportunity to tell them about His grace!

The ways that immodesty reveals its idolatrous heart are virtually endless. Any attempt to use your body to draw inappropriate attention to yourself rather than to God is immodest and worships the idol of self. You don't have to hide, but you do have to cover those God-given gifts that are meant to be revealed only to your husband. Exposing these gifts outside the context of marriage cries out for the lustful attention of guys.

Point people to God by your modest behavior and dress. King Lemuel listened to his mom. How about you? Do you trust God's Word or do you reject it? There is no middle ground!

Some Sinful Motives behind Immodesty

Pride. The opposite of fearing God is drawing attention to oneself through pride. Unfortunately, pride is an all-too-common motive behind so much of what we do. Isaiah 3:16–24 describes how pride can choose to clothe itself with immodesty. Notice especially how appropriately God's punishment fits this crime.

> Moreover, the LORD said, "Because the daughters of Zion
>   [the Jewish women] are proud,
>   and walk with heads held high and seductive eyes,
>   and go along with mincing steps,

and tinkle the bangles on their feet,
therefore the Lord will afflict the scalp of the daughters
      of Zion with scabs,
and the LORD will make their foreheads bare."
In that day the Lord will take away the beauty of their
anklets, headbands, crescent ornaments, dangling earrings,
bracelets, veils, headdresses, ankle chains, sashes, perfume
boxes, amulets, finger rings, nose rings, festal robes, outer
tunics, cloaks, money purses, hand mirrors, undergarments,
turbans and veils.
    Now it will come about that instead of sweet perfume
        there will be putrefaction [stench of rotting flesh];
instead of a belt, a rope;
instead of well-set hair, a plucked-out scalp;
instead of fine clothes, a donning of sackcloth;
and branding instead of beauty. (Isaiah 3:16–24)

God has called you, as a believer, to deny yourself (Luke 9:23) and to live your life in such a way so that He is glorified (1 Corinthians 10:31). You are not to compete with God for the glory that is rightfully due Him. While you don't need to be afraid of the particular judgments of Isaiah 3, which the Jews did experience when God sent Babylon to judge them, know that God hates pride that expresses itself in immodesty. One day God will judge these kinds of prideful expressions if they are not followed by repentance and faith in Christ.

Is the motive behind what you do or wear one that glorifies God through your humble and modest spirit, or are you trying to compete with almighty God for the attention that He rightfully deserves? Pride is a subtle, dangerous sin that manifests itself in many ways, including immodesty.

People-Pleasing. Another sinful motive behind immodesty is being a people-pleaser who is always trying to fit in with the world. Do your clothing choices and behavior show that you are a citizen of the world or a citizen of God's kingdom?

In the Old Testament, God called his nation Israel to be different, to be holy (Numbers 15:37–41), and not just to be like the nations around them. But in Zephaniah we read, "Then it will come about on the day of the LORD's sacrifice, that I will punish the princes, the king's sons, and all who clothe themselves with foreign garments" (Zephaniah 1:8). These leaders chose not to be holy. Rather than depend upon God, they imitated the idolatrous Assyrians, their very enemies. James Bruckner describes it this way: "Clothing was a symbol that people were adopting the cultural and religious values of Assyria at the expense of the worldview and faith revealed to them by the true God."[1]

What's wrong with dressing in foreign garments? Is it a sin to wear a kimono, a hula skirt, or some other piece of clothing that is not from your own culture? No! Don't throw out your Aussie oilskin jacket or your wooden shoes from Holland simply because they are from a foreign country. The issue is not the foreign clothes themselves, but the motive behind wearing such clothing.

In the cases of both the prideful Jewish women and these people-pleasing Jewish leaders, the issue wasn't so much what they were wearing, but why they were wearing it. Motives can make all the difference between pleasing the God of the universe and bringing His wrath down upon sinners.

Conclusion

So, what do your clothes say about your heart? What you wear is no accident. If you get to choose what you wear, your choice is a window into your heart. It reveals your motives. It may not reveal them clearly, but it will reveal them. Is pride or a desire to put other things before God partly what motivates you in what you do or wear? When people see what you wear, what would they conclude about the loyalties of your heart? Does your style of dress help people to understand that you are living to please your Lord and Savior? This also applies to what you say and how you act. Do your words and actions point people to God or to yourself?

Think of your heart as a sponge. What happens when it's squeezed? If your heart is full of immodesty, then immodesty will overflow into your dress, words, flirtations, and manipulations, just as the women's pride overflowed in the days of Isaiah. If the motives of your heart are not loyal to God (as in the case of the men in Zephaniah's day), then you will rebel in your heart, and that will spill over into your outward behavior. However, if the motives of your heart are like those of the excellent wife, you will show enduring beauty and charm by your fear of God.

The ultimate cure to immodesty is found in Proverbs 31:30 — fear the Lord! Grow in your knowledge of God in every way possible. Every time you open God's Word, focus on what it teaches about the character of God. The more accurate your view of God, the more accurately you will see your own sin. Hopefully, the more accurately you see your sin, the more you will be motivated to truly repent before our awesome God!

Review Questions

1. What was the worth of the excellent wife in Proverbs 31:10? How did she dress and clothe herself? See Proverbs 31:17, 31. How is her heart described in Proverbs 31:30?
2. How did Peter describe Sarah? See 1 Peter 3:5.
3. What does the "fear of God" look like in a person's life?

4. What happened to the daughters of Zion (the Jewish women) when they were proud and vain? See Isaiah 3:16–24.

5. According to the last paragraph in this chapter, what is the ultimate cure for immodesty?

5

Who Are Immodesty's Best Friends in the Old Testament?

A Word from Martha

When I was a girl growing up in a suburb of Atlanta, Georgia, I attended a public school and had many girlfriends. In fact, in the upper grade-school years and some of the middle-school years, some of us had a club. We were quite the exclusive group! You could not join our club unless you were voted in. We were all in the same grade and most of us lived on the same street. We had so much fun, especially with our once-a-month "slumber parties." We rotated from house to house, and why our parents put up with us laughing and playing games all night long, I will never know. We are all scattered now, but we do still keep up with each other. In fact, we have planned a reunion in a few weeks—which will, by the way, be in the daytime now that we're old!

I love all my old friends and I love all my new friends, but I want to tell you about one special friend that I had. We were best friends and did everything together. She was part of our club, too. She was an only child like I was. I was just as comfortable at her house as she was at mine. After high school we went to different colleges, but we still had that friendship bond. She was the maid of honor at my wedding, and six weeks later I was the matron of honor at hers. My husband and I named our first child after her. Her name is Anna.

If I had a problem, Anna knew all about it, and vice versa.

We consulted each other about everything and, of course, influenced each other in many ways. We had many secrets and could practically know what the other one was thinking or how the other one would react. We knew we could count on each other. Have you ever heard the expression, "Birds of a feather flock together"? Well, Anna and I were like that, sticking together through thick and thin.

That is how good friends are. They are faithful, and you can trust them. The Bible tells us that "a man's counsel is sweet to his friend" (Proverbs 27:9). That can certainly be good news, but it can also be bad news. Counsel from a friend influences us in many ways. It can influence us to be godly, *and* it can influence us to sin.

This book is about repenting from immodesty and becoming modest and pure in your heart and outward dress. Pastor Kent is going to explain about some "friends" that are not such good influences in your life. You could say that they are the cohorts of immodesty sticking together like birds of a feather. It is rare that you can have one without the other. Just as you hardly ever saw me as a child and teen without my friend Anna, you hardly ever see immodesty without its best friends—sensuality, shame, and seduction. My friend, Anna, was beautiful. Immodesty's friends are ugly—very ugly. Pastor Kent will explain.

A Word from Pastor Kent

You can tell a lot about a person by his or her friends. Cheerleaders tend to befriend the athletically skilled as well as those who are beautiful or handsome. Artistic people tend to hang out with others who are artistically gifted. Brainiacs generally associate with others who tend to wreck everyone else's grades when teachers grade on a curve. You get the idea. Friends normally have similar interests. They already have a lot in common, which makes it easy to be friends.

And no matter how much you and your friends have in common when the friendship first starts, the longer you hang out, the more you'll influence one another. You end up talking the same way your friends do, thinking about things more like your friends, and acting like your friends and doing the things they like to do.

We choose our friends for specific reasons, even though we may not think about those reasons very much. Sometimes parents blame their children's friends when their children are caught in sin. This makes sense on one level, as we often experiment with new and risky things because of the influence of our friends. The problem with his idea, though, is that *we* are the ones who chose these friends in the first place. There is something in our heart that desires these people to be our friends. No one can ever be your friend, or make you sin, if you don't want to do so. They may influence you, but it is from your own heart that sinful desires come (Mark 7:20–23; James 1:14). The friends whom you choose to influence you *are* a reflection of your heart's desires. (We'll spend more time later on showing what the Bible says about choosing friends.)

Therefore, it is no surprise who we find as the close friends of immodesty in the Bible. Since immodesty is a sin, we find other sins closely associated with this kind of sin. These friends are sensuality, shame, and seduction.

Immodesty's Best Friends: Sensuality

Sensuality is simply that which satisfies the senses. It doesn't have to be a sinful thing. Silk has a sensual feel that has nothing to do with sin in and of itself. Some people believe that rich European chocolate has a smooth, sensual taste. Perfume can bring about sensual connotations that are not sinful.

But usually "sensuality" is used to mean satisfying or appealing to sexual desires through the five senses. Sensuality, in the form of what you say, do, and wear, is often the reason for immodesty. It tempts the lustful person by what he hears and sees. Sensuality, in what you say (flirting by hinting at sexual themes is denounced in Ezekiel 33:31–32 and Ephesians 5:3–6) and in how you touch that cute guy, can inflame desires for what God would forbid outside marriage. That little brush of his arm or casual touch is probably saying more than you meant to say. You know you are getting his attention, but these forms of sensuality can easily appeal to sexual desires that ought not be aroused.

I believe this is the idea of 1 Corinthians 7:1, where Paul is probably quoting a common saying among the Corinthians, which warns that "it is good for a man not to touch a woman." In this passage it is the guy who is initiating, but this principle certainly applies the other way as well. The touch that is in view here is a sensual touch. (You don't need to worry about accidentally bumping into guys in the hallway.) Any touch that appeals to sexual desires is a sensual touch.

Not all touch, as you know, is sensual. It is good to appropriately express affection. The Bible encourages Christians to "greet one another with a holy kiss" (Romans 16:16).[1] Please note that this kiss needs to be "holy." This is practiced in many cultures today. In the United States, we don't tend to kiss one another as a greeting, though we do greet with hugs and handshakes. Handshakes are fine, so don't worry. However, hugs take some explanation.

Your intentions are probably good in offering or receiving a hug with a guy. It is possible that the guy's intention is good too, but typically he will be quite aware of your body being pressed against his. When girls are younger, this isn't an issue. But the more developed your body becomes, the more this becomes an issue. This can be a real temptation to guys—one that they can resist, but it isn't easy.

My recommendation is to hug guys with a side hug. If you do hug face to face, keep distance between you two so that contact is minimized. By being careful to give "holy" hugs, rather than sensual hugs, you can help guys as they face this temptation.

Sensuality is very closely related to immodesty and should be avoided. While there are many warnings against the sin of sensuality in the New Testament,[2] there are passages in the Old Testament that speak of the sin of sensuality as well.[3]

The clearest picture of sensuality is found in Ezekiel 23:1–21.[4] This is a metaphor of two women who have a sensual desire for men of royalty.[5] This sensuality expressed itself in adultery and prostitution (another friend of immodesty, according to the Bible). They should have been faithful to their husbands, but they followed their sensual desires instead. The result of following through on this sensuality was consequences that were both spiritual and physical: shame and then death.

When we ourselves give in to sinful sensuality, there are certainly physical consequences that can result for us. But, as horrible as the physical consequences are, this passage in Ezekiel warns of the spiritual dangers of sensuality—separation from God, broken relationships with others, the potential for habits of sin that become more difficult to turn from in repentance. Whenever we step outside God's boundaries for us, which are given to us for our good, we are entering a realm filled with danger. Sensuality is nothing to play around with if you care about God and yourself.

Immodesty's Best Friends: Shame

Another close friend of immodesty is not a *good* friend at all. This friend is something we tend to try to avoid at all costs. This close friend of immodesty is shame. Why anyone would want to hang around with "Shame" is beyond me! I hate the embarrassment that comes with shame—feeling my face get hot as the blood rushes to reveal to anyone who is looking that I am feeling shame. But typically in our Western culture, we don't feel shame anywhere near the degree that people experienced shame in the cultures in which the Bible's events took place. Their culture may even be described as a shame-based culture. In these cultures, death is better than experiencing shame because of how it reflects poorly on their family or community.

The normal usage of "shame" in our culture refers to an internal attitude that we feel. In the Bible, "shame" is normally used to describe public humiliation, how others think about us. Even today, many cultures use shame as a powerful motivation for good behavior.

The Bible consistently associates immodesty with shame. We saw this close association in our study of the origin of clothes. Clothes were given so that we would not feel shame due to nakedness. Public nakedness in the biblical cultures was a horrible disgrace—one to be avoided at all costs!

It is not surprising, then, that the Bible teaches a lot about nakedness, which is helpful for our understanding of modesty and immodesty. So, what does the Bible teach?

First of all, nakedness, in the context of a husband and wife in privacy, is presented as a precious gift from God to be enjoyed (see the Song of Solomon).[6] Shame should have no part in this God-glorifying context.

Outside the privacy of marriage, however, nakedness is consistently portrayed as being sinful and shameful when in public. Notice how many Old Testament passages connect nakedness with shame, such as Genesis 3:7–11; 2 Samuel 6:20; and Nahum 3:5.[7] In fact, the Hebrew word for "nakedness" can also be translated as "shame" or "indecency" in various contexts. In the Old Testament mindset, revealing parts of the body that should be covered was closely related to the shame that came with it.[8]

Second, we need to understand what the Bible means by the word "naked." We think nakedness means that someone is wearing no clothes at all. In Bible times, though, nakedness would also include what we today call immodesty. In the Old and New Testaments, people were considered naked when they had on too little clothing, because they were revealing parts of their body that were not considered modest when revealed in public.

For example,[9] in Exodus 20:26, we read that if priests wearing their priestly robes were exposed while walking up stairs, they were "naked." If people can see the parts of your body that ought to be covered, the Bible would consider you to be naked. Mini-skirts, even as their name implies, seem to qualify for this definition of biblical nakedness. If walking up stairs or having the wind blow causes problems in keeping your private parts private, you are naked according to the Bible.

Rather than putting immodesty in the category of nakedness, something that brings shame, our culture places immodesty in the category of fashion, something to be praised and imitated by others. Instead of feeling the shame they *should* feel if their consciences were trained according to the Bible, immodest people can glory in their shame. To make the situation worse, our culture not only parades its immodesty for all to see, but also gives "hearty approval to those who practice" it.

This statement, from Romans 1:32, describes the culmination of when people pursue sin so deeply that God lets them go in their pursuit of sin (Romans 1:24, 26, 28). Instead of restraining people from their sin, God lets go of them to allow them to wallow in their sinfulness—much like a pig in his mud pit. Remember the picture of a "gold ring in a pig's snout"? The pig is proud and does not know that he looks so completely out of place. That picture quite appropriately captures the utter depravity of glorifying immodesty.

The best way to avoid shame is to do nothing that is shameful. But there is another way that people try to avoid shame, and that is by ignoring the shame they should feel by searing their consciences (see 1 Timothy 4:2). If you continue to ignore your conscience when it warns you not to do what is wrong, it will stop working. At first, when you think about wearing something that might be a little risqué, you might feel nervous and wonder what people will think. But if you continue to wear immodest clothing, eventually you will not feel this same nervousness. The feeling of being nervous in this situation is your conscience trying to get you to wear something different, something modest. You know you're pushing the boundaries of what is acceptable. But after a while, the conscience quits working and you feel free to wear immodest clothing. You have succeeded in avoiding the feeling of shame. The problem is that you have seared your conscience, and it is no longer working to warn you of the shame of immodesty. This opens the door for you to pursue more sin, since there is no internal restraint of the conscience. This path will certainly lead to more sin unless repentance renews your mind and conscience.

Immodesty's Best Friends: Seduction

Immodesty's friends have led to no good. It is impossible for sinful sensuality to satisfy the godly heart, even though it lies by promising a satisfaction it can never deliver. Shame is not a friend at all, but rather an enemy. But then this is not a surprise, since we are talking about the friends of immodesty. There is one more friend frequently found associating with immodesty—seduction.

There are two categories of seduction in the Old Testament.

The professional seductress is called a prostitute. It is no surprise that, to the Jews, prostitution was a shameful activity. It wasn't simply the act of prostitution that was considered shameful. According to Proverbs, you can tell a prostitute by the shameful way she acts and dresses—her advertisements, if you will.

There is another category in the book of Proverbs, however, that is more appropriate for our purposes—the "amateur" seductress. The "amateur" seductress is not a prostitute by profession, but is someone who desires immoral relationships. In Proverbs, Solomon warns his son to avoid the woman who would try to seduce him into immorality.[10]

First of all, Solomon points out the immodesty of the seductress's flirtatious actions. In her relationship with God, she is evil (Proverbs 6:24) and a hypocrite (7:14) who forgets her covenant with God (2:17). Her immoral desire for sinful relationships exposes itself as she cunningly seduces those who are naive (7:7, 10, 21; 9:16) by being exhilarating (5:20) and using flattering words that sound so smooth and sweet (2:16; 5:3; 6:24; 7:14–21; 9:15–17), and with her eyes, which hunt down her prey (6:25–26), while she boldly initiates immoral sexual intimacy (7:13; 9:16–17).

Solomon also describes the way that this seductress dresses as a harlot, a prostitute (7:10). She dresses in such a way as to encourage and capture the interest of those who desire sexual immorality. A prostitute's style of clothing advertises her profession. A vivid example is found in Genesis 38:14–15. Tamar dressed in the distinctive way of a prostitute to capture Judah's interest so that she could manipulate him. He recognized that she was inviting him to sexual immorality simply by the way she was dressed.

It is not only prostitutes who dress seductively. Those who want power and the interest and attention of the guys they want to capture will also dress in this immodest style. Maybe you don't get the attention that your heart craves, and you desperately want guys to notice you. Immodesty, though, is not the answer!

Even if you're not trying to seduce some cute guy you know, immodesty is still an invitation to sexual immorality, whether you mean it that way or not. Immodesty *will* capture the interest of those who are interested in immorality.

At the end of his warning to his son about the seductress, Solomon states, "Her house is the way to Sheol, descending to the chambers of death" (Proverbs 7:27). Earlier in the book he describes the immoral woman this way:

> For her house sinks down to death,
> And her tracks lead to the dead;
> None who go to her return again,
> Nor do they reach the paths of life. (Proverbs 2:18–19; cf. 5:5,
>   9–14; 6:26–35)

Immodesty is playing with fire, and that fire can lead to the fire of hell for all who do not repent of sin.

Immodesty doesn't necessarily lead to sexual immorality. But immodesty *is* sometimes chosen for the purpose of sexual immorality. It is common in the Old Testament to associate immodesty with sexual immorality. Even the word "nakedness" can be a euphemism for the sexual organs of the body[11] or for sexual acts.[12] The reason this euphemism works is because of the close ties that exist between exposing one's body and sexual intimacy.

Immodesty's Friends Are *Not* Helpful Friends

One other thing to consider is this: newspapers and magazines often report on the fashion trends of the day that are constantly changing. Sometimes the changes are drastic. Even non-Christian periodicals like *Time* magazine see the fashion changes. In one of its reports on women's fashions, *Time* stated that the newest fashion strategy is modesty. In fact, it went on to report that "the super-exposure of nudity seems not to have given women much happiness."[13] I agree that it hasn't given women much happiness, but I don't agree that the new styles are modest. If they are, I don't think many women have gotten the word.

If you let fashion dictate how you dress, you will spend a fortune on these constantly changing styles. But more importantly, you will be imitating the world and not following God's Word. James 4:4 is strong in denouncing the imitation of the world. It says, "You adulteresses, do you not know that friendship with the world is hostility toward God? Therefore whoever wishes to be a friend of the world makes himself an enemy of God." Those who are friends of God will not be friends with immodesty or any of her friends, no matter what the fashionistas say.

The Old Testament is clear that where there is immodesty, there is often sensuality, shame, and seduction. They tend to spend a lot of time together and are seldom separated since they are best friends.

Immodesty is not merely a way to get attention. It is a dangerous and foolish lure that can catch unwanted attention and lead to unwanted consequences.

Review Questions

1. What is the usual meaning for the word "sensuality"?
2. According to Romans 1:24–25, what happens to people who pursue sin so deeply that God turns them over to their lusts?
3. Look up the following verses and make a list of the characteristics of the seductress: Proverbs 2:16, 17; 5:3, 6; 6:24; 7:10, 13–21, 9:13–18.

2. Match the following:

God's discipline on Nineveh that would bring shame	Ephesians 5:3-6
Sensual touches	Genesis 3:7-11
What the Priests were forbidden to do	1 Corinthians 7:1
Flirting by hinting at sexual themes	Nahum 3:5
Original sin and shame	Exodus 20:26

PART THREE

The New Testament on Immodesty

A Word from Martha

I am part of the biblical counseling team at my church. We offer free biblical counseling to the church family and the community. I mostly counsel women, but sometimes I co-counsel couples who need help. In those cases, I work with the pastor in charge of the counseling ministry.

Recently, I counseled a young woman who is struggling to obey the Lord in her role as a wife. She is working hard to understand and does have a desire to obey God. She also asks thoughtful questions. For instance, the other day, she asked, "Do you believe that women are inferior to men?" The simple answer to that question is no. I went on to explain that sometimes a woman is *superior* to a man in many ways. She may be smarter. She may be better looking. She may act like a Christian and he might not. She may keep the laws of her country and he might be a lawbreaker.

Next my counselee asked, "So then, what does the *Bible* teach about a woman being inferior to a man?" I gave her a similar answer: "The Bible teaches that men and women are equal in God's eyes. There is 'neither male nor female, for you are all one in Christ Jesus' (Galatians 3:28)." Husbands are warned to "live with your wives in an understanding way . . . and grant her honor as a *fellow heir* of the grace of life" (1 Peter 3:7). Women are creatures created in God's image just like men are. However, they do have different roles in marriage. The husband is to be the leader in the home and the wife is to be his "helper suitable" (Genesis 2:18; see also Ephesians 5:22–24). God's Word does not teach that she is inferior, but if she wants to be in God's will, she simply has a different role to fulfill.

In this part of the book, we will see what the New Testament teaches about modesty. The world, like my counselee, has many questions and misperceptions about how women are viewed by God from His Word. Similarly, the world has many questions and misperceptions about immodesty—such as why I can't wear what I want to wear, and the issue of legalism. The chapters in this section will explain the answer to many of those questions and misperceptions. Let's turn now to Pastor Kent's word to you.

A Word from Pastor Kent

Immodesty is virtually everywhere on TV. It seems as if the easiest way to sell something on TV involves a beautiful young woman acting in a flirtatious or even seductive manner. The ads tend to be even more enticing if this young woman is immodestly dressed. Unfortunately, these young women are being used to manipulate lustful desires in men. In effect, they are being reduced to an object, an image that is divorced from who they are as a person, in order to sell a product or a service.

This is nothing new. Our culture has the same problems recognizing the precious personhood of women as those cultures did in the New Testament. Several years ago, I was able to visit the ancient city of Ephesus, and carved right into the public sidewalk was an advertisement for the local brothel of the first century AD with an arrow pointing the way.

In these ancient cultures, women were considered to be only objects, possessions for men's pleasure. Because of its high regard for women, the Bible was revolutionary to the cultures of that time. The New Testament shows that God's view of women is much higher than how the world has commonly viewed women throughout history.

In the Greek, Roman, and Jewish cultures of the first century, women were viewed almost as a possession. Men could divorce their wives, but wives were not allowed to divorce their husbands. It was considered a waste to teach women the Torah (the Jewish Law). The testimony of women wasn't allowed in court since they were considered to be liars. Men wouldn't even allow women to touch them since the women might be defiled. Women had it rough!

When Jesus entered the scene, he rejected these cultural practices by honoring women. He taught women frequently (Luke 10:38–42; John 4). He touched women to heal them and allowed them to touch him (Mark 5:25–34; Luke 13:10–17). He allowed women to travel with him (Luke 8:1–3), something completely unknown by Jewish rabbis of the first century. He first revealed Himself to Mary Magdalene after His resurrection and sent her to testify of this to the disciples (John 20:1–18).[1]

Middle Eastern cultures (the cultures of the Bible) have not always been so kind to women. There is a famous prayer by a Jewish rabbi that goes like this: "God, I thank you that you did not make me a Gentile, a dog, or a woman." Women were considered to be second-class citizens. They were often regarded as a piece of property for the purpose of gratifying the sexual desires of men. In Europe, during the Middle Ages, "Medieval law declared even a noblewoman to be her father's or husband's property."[2]

Immodesty perpetuates a low view of women and contradicts God's high purposes for women. It is choosing to treat yourself as a piece of property that lust can possess, at least in the mind of any guy who chooses to store your image away. Reducing yourself to a visual memory for lustful men is not honoring to God's purposes for you. This is clear in both testaments of the Bible.

The New Testament is built upon the teaching of the Old Testament. Therefore, many of the principles of modesty found in the Old Testament will also apply to the New Testament, although some of them are transformed as they enter into the time of the New Covenant. This section explains how the New Testament principles of immodesty should be applied today in our culture. The bottom line is that the New Testament praises modesty and rejects immodesty as a sin to be wholeheartedly avoided!

6

Why Were Women Immodest in the New Testament?

A Word from Martha

Immodesty is one of those sins that are "common to man" (1 Corinthians 10:13). It was common during the Old Testament times and it is common today. Today, however, we are on the other side of the cross. What that means for us is that we now have special help to turn from our sin. You see, there were some previously hidden "mysteries" hinted at in the Old Testament that have now been revealed in the New Testament. They were revealed first to the apostles and now to us. This is what happened:

When the Lord Jesus was here on earth, He told His apostles that He would be killed and would rise again from the dead. The apostles were frightened and confused; they did not want Him to leave them. But the Lord assured them it would be *better* for them if He died and left them, because God the Father was going to send them another "Helper." That "Helper" would be the Holy Spirit. Jesus said, "You know Him because He abides with you and will be in you" (John 14:17). The Holy Spirit would also "bring to your remembrance all that I said to you" (John 14:26).

The promise of the Holy Spirit had to be comforting to the apostles, but it should also be comforting to us. Why? Because this happens to every Christian since the Lord Jesus rose from the dead and then ascended back to heaven. It was important for the disciples to be able to remember accurately what Jesus taught and did, because they were eyewitnesses. Some of them would, as a result, write the Gospels, which tell us of Jesus' life and ministry. The Holy Spirit's indwelling of believers is also important for us, because we need His help in order to live the Christian life. This includes not only our outward behavior but also our inward thoughts and the desires in our hearts.

Later on in this chapter, Pastor Kent is going to tell you what the New Testament reveals about your heart's motive. But right now I want to tell you more about the Holy Spirit's role in your life if you are a Christian.

The Holy Spirit is the third member of the Trinity—God the Father, God the Son (Jesus Christ), and God the Holy Spirit. The Holy Spirit was manifested at Jesus' baptism in the form of a dove, while the Father's voice could be heard saying of Jesus, "This is My beloved Son, in whom I am well-pleased" (Matthew 3:17).

Not long after Jesus ascended to heaven, the apostle Peter preached a very famous sermon. As thousands of people were being saved, God sent the promised "Helper" in the person of the Holy Spirit, who indwelt them and gave them new hearts (Acts 2). That way, they could love God and glorify Him. Since that time, all Christians, at the moment of their salvation, have been cleansed of their sin and given a new heart, and are indwelt by the Holy Spirit.

Our initial salvation is 100 percent the work of God. We do not deserve forgiveness, and we cannot earn it. We cannot make it happen. Instead, because of His love and mercy, God draws us to Himself, convicts us of our sin, supernaturally grants us forgiveness, and gives us credit for the righteousness of Christ. God places us in a right relationship with Himself. This is called "positional sanctification" (see, for example, Ephesians 4:24; Hebrews 10:10). To be sanctified means to be holy—that is, to be set apart from sin to a life of service to God.

At salvation, we are forgiven of all our sin, but we know that we do still commit sin. So, from the time that God saves us until the time we go to be with the Lord is what theologians call a second phase of sanctification. This phase is called "progressive sanctification" (see, for example, Philippians 2:12–13). In other words, we grow and mature as Christians, sinning less and glorifying God more and more. We are, as the apostle Paul said, "[becoming] conformed to the image of His Son" (Romans 8:29). This can happen only because of the "Helper," the Holy Spirit, who is convicting us of our sin and *helping* us to live a godly life.

So now we know why it was to the apostles' advantage and to our advantage that Jesus rose again from the dead and that He returned to heaven.

Once individuals are saved, the Holy Spirit continues to progressively change them, and this process is a work of God *and*, at the same time, an obligation for new Christians to "discipline [themselves] for the purpose of godliness" (1 Timothy 4:7).

This is what I want you to understand—you *can* grow and mature toward Christlikeness if you are a Christian. God *will* help you as you put forth effort. That is God's enabling grace. He will change your heart's motive, and you can have a great joy in pleasing Him.

Now Pastor Kent is going to tell you much more about what the New Testament reveals about your heart and the issue of modesty.

A Word from Pastor Kent

Have you ever thumbed through a catalog from your favorite clothing store and thought about what the effect would be if you wore the different outfits pictured? It is amazing how much we can communicate about ourselves by the clothing choices we make. Sometimes this is intentional, other times it might be unintentional. Whether or not we think about what messages we're communicating, what we wear always has something to say about us as people.

Why are you wearing the clothes you have on now? What reasons flashed through your mind as you selected your clothes this morning? Did you think of who you would meet today and what impression you wanted to leave on that person—maybe a guy?—by your clothing choices? What were the motives behind your choices?

Understanding the motives behind what you wear is quite helpful if you want to be modest. As I have said, it is possible to wear modest clothing and still be immodest. If your heart is immodest, you can thoroughly cover your body but still act and speak in immodest ways. The solution to immodesty is found in purifying the motives of your heart.

The tricky thing, though, is that motives are difficult to evaluate because our heart is deceitful and desperately sick (see Jeremiah 17:9). The heart is the location of our motives (1 Corinthians 4:5), and it is quite difficult to understand fully all the motives behind the choices we make. You can often determine at least some of your motives, especially if you take the time to examine them. But, ultimately, only God can completely know your motives. God says of Himself in Jeremiah 17:10, "I, the LORD, search the heart, I test the mind, even to give to each man according to his ways, according to the results of his deeds."

The psalmist didn't trust his own evaluation of his motives but asked God to examine his heart.

Search me, O God, and know my heart;
Try me and know my anxious thoughts;
And see if there be any hurtful way in me,
And lead me in the everlasting way. (Psalm 139:23–24)

You can, as Martha explained, trust the Holy Spirit to work in your heart and show you your sin. In addition, God has given us another instrument for examining the motives of our heart. God has given us a "surgeon's scalpel"[1]—the very Word of God, which is "able to judge the thoughts and intentions [read 'motives'] of the heart" (Hebrews 4:12).

When it comes to clothes, what do you want? Do you want to impress your friends? That cute guy whose locker is across the hall from you? Yourself when you ask the mirror to comment on your beauty? All the above? These motives may not necessarily be wrong.

A more helpful question regarding motives is *how* do you want to impress? What are you trying to accomplish? What are you trying to communicate about yourself? Do you want to encourage envy in your girlfriends? Do you dress immodestly to gain that cute guy's attention? Do you want everyone to see how God has formed you—not for His glory, but for your own? Immodesty is often driven by these kinds of motives and by others as well.

Do you want to show that you have respect for yourself and for others? Do you want to show that God is first in your life? If so, you will dress modestly. Psalm 149:4 teaches that God does find pleasure in His people who are satisfied in Him. Who are you dressing for?

There are many strong warnings in the New Testament against imitating the world—that is, the evil satanic system that fights against God. Deep down, a desire to be immodest is driven by a love of the world. Is that an issue for you? I hope that as you read the following passages, you will ask for God's help as you use the "surgeon's scalpel" of God's Word to reveal the motives of your heart, so that you can evaluate how modest your heart truly is!

Surgeon's Scalpel #1

> What is the source of quarrels and conflicts among you? Is not the source your pleasures that wage war in your members? You lust and do not have; so you commit murder. And you are envious and cannot obtain; so you fight and quarrel. You do not have because you do not ask. You ask and do not receive, because you ask with wrong motives, so that you may spend it on your pleasures. You adulteresses, do you not know that friendship with the world is hostility toward God? Therefore whoever wishes to be a *friend of the world* makes himself an enemy of God. (James 4:1–4)

James 4:1–4 teaches about the consequences that come from the sinful motive of wanting to please oneself instead of God. Those who were purchased by the blood of Christ and are now to be faithful to God are considered to be adulteresses against God if they choose to befriend the world. Do you dress like worldly people so that they will accept you? It is sin to love what the world says and does more than you love what God wants for you.

You are probably dressing much more modestly than some people at your school or at your local mall, but this is not the biblical measurement for modesty. The Bible never calls you to measure yourself by the world's standards, but instead to measure yourself against what God has said! Ephesians 5:1 calls us to be imitators of God. Do you follow God's desire for His children to be modest? First John 2:6 tells us to walk in the same manner as Jesus walked. Doing better than the world does not mean that you are pleasing God! For us as believers, the world is not to be our standard. God's Word is the standard by which we are to measure ourselves.

Surgeon's Scalpel #2

> I urge you therefore, brethren, by the mercies of God, to
> present your bodies a living and holy sacrifice, acceptable
> to God, which is your spiritual service of worship. And do
> not be conformed to this world, but be transformed by the
> renewing of your mind, that you may prove what the will
> of God is, that which is good and acceptable and perfect.
> (Romans 12:1–2)

Paul's letter to the church of Rome is his most comprehensive letter on the subject of salvation and the implications of what it means to be saved. The first eleven chapters help us to understand who we are in Christ. Then, in Romans 12:1, Paul begins to focus upon what we are to do because of who we are in Christ. After urging believers to offer their lives as a living sacrifice to God, Paul warns against being like the world ("And do not be conformed to this world"). The Phillips New Testament in Modern English (a paraphrase rather than a word-for-word translation) states it this way: "Don't let the world around you squeeze you into its own mould, but let God re-mould your minds from within, so that you may prove in practice that the plan of God for you is good, meets all his demands and moves towards the goal of true maturity."

If you belong to God, then you cannot fight on the side of His enemies by doing things contrary to His will! If everyone at your school, neighborhood, city, county, state, country, continent, hemisphere, planet, solar system, galaxy—you get the point—acts, talks, and dresses in a way that God says His children should not imitate, it doesn't matter. Christians live to please God!

This can be painful. Your "friends" may make fun of you for choosing to be modest. Teenagers, especially, want to belong.

But when it comes to morality, choosing right or wrong, do you want to belong to the world or to God? If you remember that the Bible continually contrasts the temporary nature of our life with the incomprehensible duration of eternity, you can find help to endure the pain of being "hated" by the world for righteousness' sake (John 15:18–21).

Loving the world is obviously wrong. Trying to love the world *and* love God is completely distasteful to our Lord! When some people tried to sit on the fence by loving the world *and* loving God, Jesus said he wanted to spit them out of His mouth. (They were "lukewarm"—see Revelation 3:16.) Only a consistent love for God (and true biblical repentance when we have loved the world) will please Him.

Surgeon's Scalpel #3

> As obedient children, do not be conformed to the former lusts which were yours in your ignorance, but like the Holy One who called you, be holy yourselves also in all your behavior; because it is written, "You shall be holy, for I am holy." (1 Peter 1:14–16)

In 1 Peter 1:14–16, Peter offers another clear perspective on this motive behind immodesty in his quotation of Leviticus 11:44. The words "in your ignorance" refer to unbelievers not being able to understand what God requires of people (1 Corinthians 2:14). Believers are not to be ignorant, since God has told us what we need to know in His Word. Therefore, if God *has* adopted you into His family, you need to follow the desires of your heavenly Father, not the worldliness that everyone is born into (Ephesians 2:1–3). Since God is perfectly holy (1 John 1:5–7), that is the standard for which we strive (Matthew 5:48). This holiness requires pure motives that seek God's glory above all things, and it expresses itself in both word and deed.

Being holy means being different. It means you are set apart for the exclusive use of your Master. Your only concern is His pleasure. Nothing else satisfies the longings of your heart. The joy of your heart is found through following God's Word. This can't be done if you allow your past habits as an unbeliever to squeeze you into the world's mold.

Are you acting and dressing to please God? Do you have a holy heart that expresses itself in modesty?

Surgeon's Scalpel #4

> Beloved, I urge you as aliens and strangers to abstain from fleshly lusts, which wage war against the soul. Keep your behavior excellent among the Gentiles, so that in the thing in which they slander you as evildoers, they may on account of your good deeds, as they observe them, glorify God in the day of visitation. (1 Peter 2:11–12)

Peter addresses our motives again in 1 Peter 2:11–12. You are not to belong to this world. You are an alien and a stranger—though not from outer space. No, you are from much farther away than that—you are a citizen of heaven (Philippians 3:20).

I was born in Illinois but had the pleasure of being a youth pastor in Australia for five years. After being there for a few years, I really wanted to fit in. I remember thinking that I had paid my dues by living there for years and should now be accepted into the culture there. I had permanent residence status and planned on living there for the rest of my life. When I would call home to the States, people were impressed with how Australian I sounded. Yet every time I opened my mouth, Aussies would recognize that

I was an American. It was uncomfortable being different, but I couldn't do much about it. I foolishly tried to imitate their accent, which was always good for a laugh but didn't actually help.

God said, through Peter, that you are to be different and even to be thrilled with being different because joy comes from pleasing God. It may be hard at times, especially when you are persecuted for loving God. But blessed are those who are persecuted for righteousness' sake (Matthew 5:10–12). Great assurance of salvation comes when your love for God enables you to resist compromising with the world.

This truth delivers you from trying to fit into the world's sinful patterns so obviously manifested in immodesty. For example, when advertisements call a blouse a "lingerie top," this might be a good clue that it is immodest. "Undergarments" should not become outer garments. Dress in such a way that your modest lifestyle and clothing will even cause unbelievers to glorify God for your testimony to them (Matthew 5:16).

Surgeon's Scalpel #5

> Do not love the world, nor the things in the world. If anyone
> loves the world, the love of the Father is not in him. For all
> that is in the world, the lust of the flesh and the lust of the
> eyes and the boastful pride of life, is not from the Father, but
> is from the world. And the world is passing away, and also its
> lusts; but the one who does the will of God abides forever.
> (1 John 2:15–17)

Anything that promotes the "lust of the flesh and the lust of the eyes" is not from God but from the world.

In 1 John 2:15–17, the apostle John adds to what Paul and Peter have written. You are not to "love the world, nor the things in the world." How do you know what is meant by "the world" and "the things in the world"? I've heard this passage used to denounce all kinds of things because they were first invented by nonbelievers—certain styles of music, literature, media, and other things. That's not what John means here.

He tells us what he means. Measuring worldliness in 1 John 2:15–17 has nothing to do with who originated or invented something. It has everything to do with the *results*. Worldliness will inflame "the lust of the flesh and the lust of the eyes and the boastful pride of life." The result of worldly things is that they encourage lust and pride. This lust can be in you or in others.

Immodesty is worldly because the desire to draw attention to the body is often caused by a proud, sinful lust in one's heart. This desire is for something that God says is not good. Immodesty is also worldly because it incites lust in anyone who is tempted to sin against God, you, and his own spouse (either present or future) by lusting after you.

Before reading this book, you may have been naïve regarding this issue. You may not have understood what is at stake. If your heart is not modest and you speak, dress, or act immodestly, then you are responsible in part for the worldliness you incite in others, which is just what John is warning about in this passage.

If, however, you dress modestly, speak modestly, and act modestly, you aren't responsible for anyone's sin of lust against you.

Conclusion

God wants something far better for women than what the world desires. Rather than regarding women as a piece of property, God values women. Don't retreat to the pagan view that sees women as possessions for satisfying the desires of others. You were created for so much more than that!

God's Word reveals the motives of our heart, like spiritual

open-heart surgery. We may not like the motives that God's scalpel reveals to us. The conviction of sin from the Holy Spirit does not feel good. But these are God's precious gifts to believers, so that we can repent of our sin, please Him, and experience what is good for us!

Review Questions

1. Why did Jesus tell His apostles that it was better for them that He should die instead of stay there with them?
2. Why is it important that the Holy Spirit should indwell every believer?
3. What does the word "sanctified" mean?
4. Write out 1 Timothy 4:7.
5. How does Jeremiah 17:9 describe our hearts? Who can *really* know our motives? See Jeremiah 17:10.
6. Match the following:

Friend of the world	1 Peter 1:14–16
"Be holy in all your behavior"	1 John 2:15–17
Do not love the things of the world	Romans 12:1–2
Abstain from fleshly lusts	1 Peter 2:11–12
Not be conformed to this world	James 4:1–4

7. What does it mean to "not love the things of this world"?

7

What's Wrong with Being Immodest?

A Word from Martha

The other day, eight of my grandchildren stayed with a babysitter in the home of our daughter and son-in-law. Our daughter and son and their spouses were attending a conference at our church. I heard later that one of the games some of the children played was "dress up." One of the older girls, Kaylyn, applied quite a lot of makeup to the two youngest girls, Kylee and Emma. Apparently it was an amazing scene when the parents arrived home! I would have included a picture for you to see, but, sadly, the parents did not take a picture. Instead, they told them to go immediately and wash their faces. Even so, I'm glad the children had fun while it lasted.

What was little-girl fun certainly attracted the attention of everyone who saw them. Little girls giggle, laugh, and play for fun. But what about teenage and older girls who overdo their makeup or dress in a provocative way to attract attention? This really is a matter between them and God.

The Scriptures tell us about a truly beautiful woman who is described as "precious in the sight of God" (1 Peter 3:4). Her outward adornment is not overdone or sensual. The reason? She has a "gentle and quiet spirit" (1 Peter 3:4). A "gentle and quiet spirit" does *not* mean that you whisper when you talk. It *does* mean that you are humbly submitting to God and resting in His promises. In other words, it is your joy to please Him, and as a consequence you accept God's dealings with you as good.

It does not make you angry that you cannot dress the way the world dresses. Applying your makeup and getting dressed makes your heart glad when you think that you are doing it for the Lord. His commands are not a burden for you but are your joy. You are, in your heart, dressing before an audience of One—the Lord God Almighty.

He created you; He has given you "everything pertaining to life and godliness" (2 Peter 1:3) if you are a Christian. He has given you blessing upon blessing—your parents, your family, your friends, your church, your food, your education, your home, and forgiveness of your sin if you belong to Him. He has even given you freedom to enjoy makeup and stylish clothing. Enjoy it, of course! But do dress for Him.

Pastor Kent is now going to explain the main teaching on immodesty in the New Testament. When I want someone to pay attention to what I am about to say, I first say, "Now listen . . ." What he is going to teach you is very important. So, ladies, "*Now listen . . .*"

A Word from Pastor Kent

Sometimes a distraction can be a good thing. It can bring a much-needed change of pace for those who tend to focus too much or too long. My chiropractor tells me not to sit for too long in the same position if I don't want to mess up my back. Distractions remind me to get up and walk around so that my back doesn't hurt. Another helpful distraction can be background music that helps to block out unwanted noises. Familiar music can be a help to cover over other interruptions.

Normally, though, I don't like distractions, and it seems that there are endless ways to be distracted. Loud or unusual noises often distract. Daydreams can distract you from the "joy" of homework—or from listening to your teacher or the sermon in church. Distractions in the middle of prayer can sidetrack you into thinking about any number of things so that you are no longer praying. How often have your friends distracted you with a simple text message? Distractions aren't necessarily wrong. But they can be a challenge to overcome when you are trying to concentrate on something else.

For a guy, there are few distractions in life that are more powerful than an immodestly dressed woman. (Men can also be distracted by beautiful women who are modest, but that wouldn't be your fault!) Since Jesus sends Christians "into the world" (John 17:18), Christian guys need to be prepared constantly to respond to immodesty in ways that honor God. They *should* be able to rest from this constant vigilance when they gather with their brothers and sisters in church to worship God. Here, of all places, there should be no immodesty.

Paul wrote a letter to help his spiritual son, Timothy, correct some significant problems in the church at Ephesus. This church was very dear to Paul since he had spent three years there developing close relationships with the people (Acts 20:17–38). He even wrote a book of the Bible to this church—Ephesians. Among many significant elements he addresses of the relationships of those in the church, Paul teaches them how to deal with various distractions.

He begins chapter 2 of his first letter to Timothy by challenging the men to pray, and then he turns his attention to those women who were a sinful distraction.[1]

> Likewise I want women to adorn themselves with proper
> clothing, modestly and discreetly, not with braided hair and
> gold or pearls or costly garments; but rather by means of

good works, as befits women making a claim to godliness.
(1 Timothy 2:9–10)

Melody Green, the wife of musician Keith Green, alludes to this verse in her pamphlet "Uncovering the Truth about Modesty."[2] She says,

> Essentially, the Scripture in 1 Timothy says that it's all right to dress however you want to, unless you are *making a claim to godliness*. In that case, the way that you dress (along with the rest of your life) must be subject to the guidelines and control of the Holy Spirit.

In Paul's eyes, claiming the name of Christ means that Christ has a claim on your life—and that means immodesty is not an option. This leads us to the first principle of this passage.

A Command, Not Merely an Opinion

In case you think that 1 Timothy 2:9–10 is just Paul's opinion that you don't need to follow, please understand that the Holy Spirit Himself inspired Paul to write exactly what he wrote. Another apostle, Peter, explained it this way:

> But know this first of all, that no prophecy of Scripture is a matter of one's own interpretation, for no prophecy was ever made by an act of human will, but men moved by the Holy Spirit spoke from God. (2 Peter 1:20–21)

In other words, this is not merely Paul's opinion. This is God's command!

Even as men are commanded to pray, women are commanded to dress appropriately. Obviously prayer is a significant part of the Christian life. Therefore it might seem strange to move from prayer to modesty, but as commentator Donald Guthrie writes, "Paul was shrewd enough to know that a woman's dress is a mirror of her mind."[3] What were the women of Paul's day thinking when they came to church dressed like the pagan women of the world? Whom did they *really* come to worship and call attention to?

Paul paints five descriptions of how God wants women to dress or, as he puts it, "to adorn themselves." The word "adorn" comes from the Greek word which is the foundation of our English words "cosmos" or "cosmetic." It means to put in order, arrange, make ready, or decorate.[4] This is a positive command for women to display their hearts' beauty in how they dress, and Paul provides excellent guidelines for you to keep in mind when you face your closet each morning with that never-ending question, "What will I wear?" You should dress (1) with proper clothing, (2) modestly, (3) discreetly, (4) not with outrageous adornment that distracts, but (5) with good works.

Proper clothing. The word "proper" is related to the word for "adorn." The idea is that proper clothing brings order by preventing the chaos of immodesty (improper clothing). Let me tell you, immodesty creates chaos in the mind of a guy who gives into the temptation to lust. When the lust of his heart latches on to the immodesty of a young woman, all other thoughts shut down as lust reigns supreme. Talk about a distraction! Proper clothing helps to curb chaos.

In this passage the word "clothing" not only refers to clothes but also includes one's "look" or demeanor.[5] It also refers to how one behaves.[6] Paul's concern is that a woman's appearance should be *appropriate* for the worship of God. For her to dress in an *improper* way, by either being seductive or showing off her wealth, would be completely *in*appropriate. Immodesty steals the glory and attention that belongs to God alone by distracting others from God-glorifying thoughts.

It is good to dress in ways that reflect attention to God for the beauty He has given you. This is done by covering that which would be distracting. Dress *properly* in order to enhance the feminine beauty that God has blessed you with in a way that does not distract from the praise of God.

Modestly. This term refers to sexuality.[7] Modesty involves a hatred for that which is sinful, so that one's actions and appearance demonstrate the dignity appropriate for a child of God. As with the description "proper clothing," "the word 'modest' does not only refer to the cut of the dress but to the attitude of the one wearing it."[8]

Modesty goes hand in hand with humility. It desires for others to focus upon the character of God. At its core is the avoidance of shame—the humiliation of immodesty. That is why the King James Version of the Bible translates this word as "shamefacedness." A godly woman would be ashamed and feel guilt if she distracted someone from worshiping God or contributed to someone's lustful thoughts by being immodest. A woman characterized by this attitude will dress so as not to be the source of any temptation. The word also has the connotation of rejecting anything dishonorable to God. "A godly woman hates sin so much that she would avoid anything that would . . . [encourage] sin in anyone."[9]

Discreetly. The third description is "discreetly" and also is a term that has primarily sexual connotations. To be discreet means being able to hide what needs to be hidden from others. For example, when we use discreet language, we use veiled terms so that we won't teach children about things they do not need to know about yet. The Bible often uses discreet language when speaking about sexual intimacy, as Song of Solomon so appropriately shows.

In terms of modesty, one is discreet when that which is private is kept private. The meaning in this context is self-control, especially regarding sexuality. Women show control by hiding their sensuality so as not to encourage lust in others.[10] You can do this by covering the precious "gifts" that you might someday present to your husband for him to unwrap in purity. All who see you will not be distracted from praising God when you dress properly.

Without being a distraction. Paul mentions some specific ways the women in the Ephesian church were being immodest. He tells them to not adorn themselves "with braided hair and gold or pearls or costly garments." What Paul meant back then is not typically what we mean today. Paul is not against braids, pearls, or even expensive clothing, per se. The closest our culture comes to what Paul is denouncing is the red carpet walk of an award show. The women are often covered with jewelry and dresses that cost more than the houses many Americans live in.

The women at Ephesus were dressing outrageously! They were braiding gold, pearls, and other jewels into their hairdos to advertise how wealthy or beautiful they were. (How much hairspray did they have to use to get it all to stand up?) They were going to church, but it may as well have been an award show; they had all eyes on them! This form of immodesty is a distraction to men *and* women.

Paul is not teaching that braids or jewelry are wrong. He is teaching that braiding a treasure into your hair is a sinful distraction. It is fine to wear a strand of pearls or golden jewelry that is modest and appropriate instead of outlandishly distracting (Genesis 24:53; Song of Solomon 1:10–11; 4:9; Isaiah 61:10).

First Timothy 2:9 teaches that women are to arrange their appearance so that it won't distract others. You don't have to walk around all day ignoring, and asking others to ignore, the bed-head that you woke up with this morning. Please arrange your hair, jewelry, and clothes in beautiful ways; just don't be distracting in how you do it. Your hairdo or necklace shouldn't keep others from focusing on God!

The apostle Peter echoes Paul's teaching in 1 Peter 3:3-4:

> And let not your adornment be merely external—braiding the hair, and wearing gold jewelry, or putting on dresses; but let it be the hidden person of the heart, with the imperishable quality of a gentle and quiet spirit, which is precious in the sight of God.

Peter's point is that your beauty should depend not upon your external appearance but upon a godly heart that loves Jesus!

We can assume that these apostles were not against wearing dresses but against wearing dresses that cost more than the annual gross domestic product of a small country. Some wealthy women's dresses were made of gold and silver thread that had pearls and jewels sewn into the garment. They were a walking fortune. Pliny the Elder[11] reported that Lollia Paulina, one-time wife of the Roman Emperor Caligula, had a dress worth more than one million dollars by today's standards. It was covered with emeralds and pearls, and she carried the receipts with her to prove its value.

Wealthy people in ancient times could dress in a style that was impossible for a poor person to match—in contrast with today, where good clothing is affordable for most people in our Western society. A costly dress worn by a wealthy woman of Paul's day could cost up to 7,000 denarii. One denarius was a day's wage for the average laborer. Thus, 7,000 denarii equaled 22 1/3 years' worth of work for the average person. When a woman entered a worship service wearing such a dress, she caused a sensation, potentially disrupting the entire service.

The church gathers to celebrate our unity in Christ (Ephesians 4:4–6), to worship God, and to make our hearts, by His grace, more beautiful for Him. Because of who we are in Christ, dressing in a way that cries out, "I am better than you," has no part in the Christian's life—any day of the week!

Practically, though, it can be a challenge to dress in a way that does not distract others. How do you know when you are inappropriately drawing attention to yourself rather than simply being as beautiful as is appropriate? As we saw in the last chapter, the best way to decide what is appropriate is to measure the motives of your heart. Questions that might be helpful are:

- Is my appearance tempting other women to envy me or my wealth?
- Do I encourage other women to feel shame since they can't afford to dress like I do?
- Am I trying to compete with other women who dress "well"?
- Do I feel that I need to spend more money to get the "right" wardrobe than would be wise, in terms of the priorities that God has given me?
- Am I trying to attract the sexual attention of men?

Depending upon your external appearance rather than on a godly heart for beauty is placing your hope in the wrong place. God's focus and your eternal destination are based upon the condition of your heart. When your heart seeks after God's glory, so will your appearance!

Good works. Finally, Paul's fifth description shows that modesty is much more than a change of clothes. It also includes our "good works." This last point is also repeated by Paul in his instructions to Titus. Paul tells him that "Older women likewise are to . . . encourage the young women to love their husbands, to love their children, to be sensible, pure, workers at home, kind, being subject to their own husbands, so that the word of God will not be dishonored. Likewise . . . in all things show yourself to be an example of good deeds" (Titus 2:3–7).

Here are some questions that will help you to follow Paul's teaching today:

- Do you spend so much time getting your appearance ready for the day that you run out of time to get your heart ready?
- Does your beauty only shine through your appearance, or does it also, and more importantly, shine through good deeds that show a love for God and others before yourself?
- Do you work at good deeds as much as or more than you work on choosing just the right clothes, jewelry, and makeup?
- Do you rejoice more in being complimented about your beauty than in being recognized for a good deed performed in humble service to God?

Paul's reference to good works shows that modesty is more than just what one wears. Modesty includes what we do, say, and think. Biblical modesty does not teach that you must dress in an ugly way or be out of fashion. Be beautiful, but be modest in the presentation of your beauty!

The title of this chapter is "What's Wrong with Being Immodest?" The answer is, it is a sin against God! Please do not take this lightly. God demands that a woman be modest. Society says that a woman is to be "liberated," "free," and "self-expressive." You have to decide whether you are going to obey this command of God and be right with Him, or conform to the world.

Review Questions

1. List the characteristics of proper adornment found in 1 Timothy 2:9–10.
2. According to 2 Peter 1:20–21, do you think that Paul simply expressed his *own* opinion when he wrote Ephesians?
3. "Proper clothing" includes more than just what you wear. What else does it include?
4. Why does the King James Version of the Bible translate "modest" with the word "shamefacedness" in 1 Timothy 2:9?
5. Is Peter telling us in 1 Peter 3:3–4 that we can never wear jewelry? Why or why not?
6. There is a list of helpful questions in bullet points near the end of this chapter for you to ask yourself. Re-read them and answer these questions. Afterward, pray and ask God to make you truly beautiful in His eyes.

8

Am I Free to Choose What I Want to Wear?

A Word from Martha

Do you know what a fork in the road is? You will most likely come upon one driving down an unpaved country road. The road is going straight and then you come upon the fork. From above, the road looks like a Y. Suppose you know that both ways ultimately end up at your destination and both take the same length of time. They are, however, different. One way goes by a beautiful lake with swans gliding across it and otters playfully splashing each other. The other way goes through a beautiful rainforest with exotic birds and monkeys in the trees. So, which way will you go? There is not a right or wrong way. They are both good.

Christians, when confronted with such a choice, have an expression: "I have freedom in the Lord to choose." So, have fun—do you want to see the swans and otters, or the birds and monkeys? Either way, it makes no difference to your Christian witness or your spiritual well-being. You have freedom in the Lord, so enjoy the ride.

Christians throughout the world have grown up in pagan places where the people around them (and they themselves, originally) worshiped idols. When they did become Christians, it did not take long to figure out that idol worship was bad. God's Word clearly says,

> You shall have no other gods before Me. You shall not make
> for yourself an idol, or any likeness of what is in heaven above
> or in the earth beneath or in the water under the earth. You
> shall not worship them or serve them, for I, the LORD your
> God, am a jealous God. (Exodus 20:3–5)

Many former idol-worshipers who became Christians wanted absolutely nothing to do with anything associated with idols. That included leftover meat that had been sacrificed to idols. The stronger, more mature Christians did not have a problem eating meat sacrificed to idols because they knew that idols were nothing. In contrast, the weaker Christians wanted to have nothing to do with such meat. In other words, some believed that they could eat the meat, while others were appalled by the idea. Some believed that they had "freedom in the Lord," but others believed it was a sin.

The apostle Paul clearly taught that Christians have freedom to eat meat, but he was concerned with not confusing or hurting those who were weaker in this area. Paul explained,

> Now we who are strong ought to bear the weaknesses of
> those without strength and not just please ourselves. Let
> each of us please his neighbor for his good, to his edification.
> (Romans 15:1–2)

Apparently it was inconvenient, at times, to find meat that had *not* been sacrificed to idols. However, Paul's attitude was, "But we endure all things, that we may cause no hindrance to the gospel of Christ" (1 Corinthians 9:12).

Eating meat sacrificed to idols was a hugely controversial matter among Christians, but Paul had the attitude of the Lord—to put other people ahead of himself. He sought "the profit of the many" (1 Corinthians 10:33). To others, he wrote, "Let no one seek his own good, but that of his neighbor" (1 Corinthians 10:24). He prayed for the people,

> Now may the God who gives perseverance and encourage-
> ment grant you to be of the same mind with one another
> according to Christ Jesus; that with one accord you may
> with one voice glorify the God and Father of our Lord Jesus
> Christ. (Romans 15:5–6)

Even though Paul's example was about giving up your free-dom in the Lord by not eating meat sacrificed to idols, the principle applies to other areas of your life. Pastor Kent will now explain.

A Word from Pastor Kent

When it comes to cars, there are only a few areas in which owning and driving a car becomes a moral issue. You need to obey the driving laws (Romans 13:1–7). You need to exercise good stewardship in how much you pay for a car. These are moral issues in which you don't have freedom to disobey or be a poor steward.

You have much freedom, though, to make many of the choices about what car you would buy. What make and model you choose is not a moral issue in and of itself. You have freedom in what color the car is. You can choose how much of a tint you want to your windows, as long as you don't choose a darker tint than the law allows.

You have a lot of freedom in how you drive a car as well. How fast you accelerate up to the speed limit (as long as you are not considered to be drag racing) is often determined not by right and wrong but by personal preferences. What station you play on the radio is up to you as long as what you are listening to honors God, does not incite you to disobey your parents, and doesn't distract you into driving in a dangerous way. If you are honoring God through your car choice and how you drive, then you have absolute freedom.

The same is true for modesty.

Within the moral boundaries of what God says is permissible in His Word, you have freedom to wear what you want to wear, say what you want to say, and act like you want to act. Many, however, if not most immodest girls *abuse* their freedom by dressing and acting according to their own desires. From God's perspective, they are actually enslaved to sin as they commit sin against Him and others. If you are a Christian, you are no longer a slave to sin but a slave to righteousness (Romans 6:15–23).

The abuse of freedom is not a new problem or even an uncommon one. It was a significant issue for the early church. In fact, Paul spends a total of five chapters on this one subject alone—which is especially noteworthy when you consider that ten of the twenty-seven New Testament books are shorter than five chapters altogether! In Romans 14–15 and 1 Corinthians 8–10 he provides many principles to help Christians to be joyful by not abusing their legitimate freedoms in Christ.

The use of freedom is meant to produce joy in our lives! As long as we stay within God's boundaries for what is right, we can enjoy our freedoms. Our good and wise God truly does know what is best for us. Sin, which brings guilt and regret, comes when we step out of bounds and into areas that God forbids for His children. When we act as if we are still slaves to sin, we forfeit the joy that God desires for us.

I would like to use the word "JOY" as an acronym to describe how you can use your freedoms in a way that honors God, benefits others, and brings true joy into your life. You have freedom if you follow the simple concept of "JOY": Jesus, Others, Yourself.[1]

"J": Jesus and Your Freedoms

When you are making any one of your seemingly millions of daily decisions regarding modesty, remember first of all that, if you are a Christian, you have a Lord who has saved you and set you free from your slavery to sin: Jesus Christ!

Remembering *whose* you are will help you to make decisions that honor Him—the One who owns all the rights of your existence. Being a Christian means that you follow Jesus Christ's leadership in your life. As we saw in our last chapter, Jesus wants you to be a modest woman! His command is unmistakable! You are free to make any choices that fall within the realms of the freedom that He has given to you.

When you make sure to honor Jesus first in your freedoms, you will find help to understand your motives as well. You can dress and act modestly, but if you do so out of pride or other sinful motives, you are not pleasing Jesus. Modesty on the outside doesn't always mean modesty on the inside. The Lord knows our hearts and isn't satisfied with only partial obedience to His Word.

Therefore, use your freedoms in a way that honors Jesus, and you will have joy!

"O": Others and Your Freedoms

What does it mean to "use your freedoms in a way that honors Jesus" in terms of how you dress? One common meaning is to dress in a way that doesn't become a "stumbling block" to *others*. This is the essence of Romans 14–15 and 1 Corinthians 8–10.

As Martha wrote at the beginning of this chapter, the issue in both of these passages was eating meat that had previously been offered to idols. Christians were free to eat this meat as long as it didn't cause other *Christians* to sin by going against their consciences in imitating those who ate this meat (Romans 14:13–23; 1 Corinthians 8:1–13) or cause *unbelievers* to question the

Christianity of those who ate meat offered to idols (1 Corinthians 10:23–33). Even though they had this freedom, they had to be careful in how they used this freedom so that they would not cause others to stumble into sin.

Again, the same is true with modesty. You have many freedoms in choosing the style, the color, the kind of material, the accessories, and how to put it all together. It is crucial, though, to use your freedoms in a way that will not cause others to stumble. And remember, modesty is more than just a change of clothes. It requires a modest heart.

I would like to substitute "food" with "clothes" in Romans 14:15 to help you to see how crucial this is. "For if because of [clothes] your brother is hurt, you are no longer walking according to love. Do not destroy with your [clothes] him for whom Christ died." "Destroy" is a really strong term, but Paul says that is exactly what you are doing to your brother when you use your freedoms in such a way that tempts him to stumble. In 1 Corinthians 8:11, Paul puts it this way: "For through your knowledge he who is weak is *ruined*, the brother for whose sake Christ died." Jesus died to set us free from sin. When you make immodest choices, you are ruining your brother in Christ (that is, anyone who is a fellow Christian)—the very one for whom Jesus died! This is not some little matter. The next verse says that you "sin against Christ" when you sin against other Christians by using your freedoms in sinful ways (1 Corinthians 8:12).

If you make immodest choices and others choose to sin by lusting over you, you are sinning by being a stumbling block. Will guys be tempted to stumble into lust because your clothes are too tight, too little, too thin, or any other "too" of immodesty? If you are showing off what should be hidden, you could also be a stumbling block to those women who become envious of how God has made you. If younger girls, who look up to you and want to be just like you, decide to dress immodestly by following your example, you are teaching them to be immodest.

Being a stumbling block is so serious that Paul was committed to give up his freedom for as long as he lived to avoid tempting a "brother to stumble" (1 Corinthians 8:13). I hope and trust that this is your commitment, too, as you honor Jesus your Lord and don't cause others to stumble in your use of freedom.

"Y": Yourself and Your Freedoms

This will probably be your favorite of the three requirements for "JOY." Once you make choices that honor Jesus and help others not to stumble, you can choose how you would like to use your freedoms! You can choose how long your sleeves are, what colors you want to go with your shoes, or what shoes you want to go with what colors. How fashionable you want to be is up to you, as long as you honor Jesus and others in your choices.

It is crucial to keep these principles in their proper order. Don't consider your own desires until you have considered what pleases Jesus first of all (Matthew 6:33). That will help you to think rightly about all the other factors in this use of freedom.

If you are not sure what honors Jesus and helps others not to stumble, then Romans 14:22–23 is very important. Paul says,

> The faith which you have, have as your own conviction before God. Happy is he who does not condemn himself in what he approves. But he who doubts is condemned if he eats, because his eating is not from faith; and whatever is not from faith is sin.

Applied to modesty, *you* must be convinced that your choices are modest. Our conscience is a valuable ally in the fight against sin. We weaken or silence our conscience when we ignore it and go against it. If you are uncertain about whether or not a choice is modest, you need to choose something else. It would be a sin to choose an outfit that you have doubts about. You need to be convinced that all your choices are modest!

Conclusion

Keep Jesus first in your decisions regarding what you are free to wear. Then, when you remember that He is your Lord and the Master over your choices and motives, think through how your decisions will affect others. Once you have determined that your freedoms honor your Lord and will not be a stumbling block for others, enjoy what pleases *you*.

This doesn't apply only to clothes. It applies to all areas in which Jesus has given us freedom to enjoy what He has provided! Keep these principles in this order, and your freedoms will bring JOY to *J*esus, *O*thers, and *Y*ou!

Review Questions

1. Even though the apostle Paul knew that he could eat meat sacrificed to idols, why did he decide *not* to do it?
2. What are the five chapters in the Bible where the apostle Paul wrote about our "freedoms in the Lord"?
3. What does the acrostic JOY stand for?
4. Write out Romans 14:15 and substitute the word "clothes" for "food."
5. What might happen to a weaker brother if you use your "freedoms" in a way that would cause him or her to stumble? See 1 Corinthians 8:11–12 and Romans 14:15.
6. What should you do if you are not certain whether or not a choice is modest?

9

How Can I Avoid Legalism in Modesty?

A Word from Martha

When I was a little girl, I remember standing in the hallway of the large church that we were members of at the time and reading what was posted on the bulletin board. One of the posts was a list of which restaurants in our area we were allowed to eat in and which ones we were not. The ones we could *not* eat at offered alcoholic beverages on the menu. It did not seem to matter if you did not even plan to drink alcohol; you simply could not go to the restaurant. The list was signed by the elders.

I did not think much about that—after all, I was just a little girl—but my parents thought it was ridiculous. We did not go out to eat very much due to the cost, and my parents did not drink much at all, but they did take me to whatever restaurants they wanted. And they enjoyed themselves. Looking back on my time at that church, there were other extra-biblical rules and regulations that the elders believed made one a good Christian.

If some of those elders had known where my parents were eating, they would have assumed that my parents were not Christians. Those elders, like the Pharisees in Jesus' day, judged others by their outward behavior. In other words, they judged other people's Christianity by the rules that they made up. That is legalism.

The funny thing is, neither my parents nor I really knew the

Lord at that time in our lives; but we thought we were Christians. We did faithfully go to church, and my Dad was a deacon. He was also president of his Sunday school class, and my Mother sang in the choir. The truth be known, we had some outward form of religion; but our hearts were far from God.

It was much later in our lives that God saved us. I was thirty-three years old; Mother was in her sixties; Dad was at the ripe old age of eighty-nine! God gave us a heart for Him! None of us based our Christianity on what restaurant we ate in.

Pastor Kent is going to explain what is wrong with legalism and how it relates to the issue of modesty. Legalism is difficult to explain, but he does a really good job.

A Word from Pastor Kent

Some things are just plain hard to define, let alone to describe in a way that people will clearly understand. Legalism is like that. It would be easier to go to your refrigerator, grab a handful of Jell-O, and squeeze it as tightly as you can without letting any of it squish out between your fingers.

Let me give you a few examples of how slippery legalism can be. Is it a sin for guys to swim with girls? How about if they are wearing those swimsuits that people wore in the year 1900 (you know, the ones that covered everything but your feet, hands, neck, and head)? Is it immodest if a neckline is lower than four fingers below the collarbone? What about girls wearing jeans—is that immodest? Are clothes loose enough if they have two inches of extra material around the chest and hips? What measurements can be used to prevent immodesty? Are dress codes good or bad? The list can go on and on, but hopefully you get the point. Bible-believing Christians answer these questions differently, especially from one culture to another. Knowing where the line of legalism starts can be exceedingly tricky.

After spending some time thinking about how to describe the various forms in which slippery legalism takes shape, I believe that math might be a helpful way to describe legalism. I realize that people tend to either love math or hate it. If you love math, this should make the whole subject of legalism easier to understand, and you can skip the next paragraph.

If you hate math, please don't practice your basketball skills by throwing this book at the closest garbage can before giving me a chance to explain. I don't plan for you to do any math in this chapter. Does that help? The words "calculus" and "trigonometry" will never again come up in this chapter. In fact, I will use only three concepts from the world of math to help describe legalism. Also, since legalism is a sinful way of trying to please God, if you apply your hatred of math to your hatred of legalism, then you will be able to avoid the pitfalls of legalism that much easier. So are you okay with a few concepts from math to help you understand and hate the sin of legalism?

There are at least three ways that legalism expresses itself. There is the legalism of addition, the legalism of subtraction, and the legalism of algebra. Are you curious yet?

The Legalism of Addition

Legalism by addition is probably the most common type of legalism addressed in the Bible. Paul wrote about this directly in 1 Corinthians 4:6 and commanded the church there "not to exceed what is written." It is so easy to add to God's Word. The motives for this can even be well meaning. In an effort not to disobey God, we add additional commands that will keep us from ever getting near disobedience, or so some think. Even this is not wrong, if we view these additional commands correctly. The error comes when we equate our additions with God's commands or when we believe that we have to obey our higher standards in order not to sin. This is adding to God's Word, a sin to be avoided!

The clearest expression of legalism by addition in the Bible is found in the legalism of the Pharisees. The strongest words of judgment that Jesus ever spoke were against these Jewish religious leaders (e.g., Matthew 23). They tried to put a fence of laws around God's law to keep themselves and others from disobeying Him. They thought that if a person never crossed the fence, then he would never disobey the law. In time, the fence became equated with God's law—or possibly became even more important than His law. The fence is not the problem. The problem is elevating the fence to the same level as the law.

For example, God commanded the Israelites to "Remember the sabbath day, to keep it holy" (Exodus 20:8–11). One of many applications of this verse that the Pharisees taught was that you couldn't spit on the Sabbath. When the spittle hit the dust, it rolled up the dust at the edges of the spittle, and that was considered to be plowing. Since plowing is work, and people were not to work on the Sabbath, these legalistic Pharisees taught that spitting violates the Sabbath command—even if a fly flies right into your mouth.

On one occasion, the Pharisees accused Jesus' disciples of disobeying "the traditions of the elders" (Mark 7:1–5). Jesus responded by teaching that man's traditions must never become more important than God's Word (Mark 7:6–13). There is nothing wrong with having traditions per se. The problem comes when we elevate our traditions to be equal to, or even above, God's Word.

God alone has the right to establish what is right and wrong. He repeatedly states in His Word that we are not to add to what He has said (Deuteronomy 4:2; 12:32; Proverbs 30:6; Revelation 22:18–19). There is nothing wrong, however, with having *personal* standards, such as not wearing shorts, always wearing sleeves, avoiding two-piece swimsuits, and so on. (I am not encouraging these commitments. I just wanted to give you some possible examples.) This isn't adding to God's Word or making our own traditions equal to Scripture, if we keep those necessary distinctions clear. So understand the difference between your *application* of Scripture and Scripture itself.

Sometimes others set the standards for what we can and cannot wear. It is common for various institutions to require dress codes for those attending their institution. These codes are found in the workplace, on some college campuses, in schools, and in many other places. They can be simple, or they can be exceedingly detailed. Various places that do this have different goals they are trying to accomplish—encouraging professionalism, preventing violence by not wearing gang colors, or fighting immodesty.

Are dress codes good or bad? We may not like them, but that doesn't make them bad. Codes may prevent certain sinful tendencies, but that does not make them good. External methods by themselves will fail to address the heart and will never reach the core of the problem. After all, modesty is more than just a change of clothes. We avoid legalism as long as we keep dress codes on a separate level under the authority of God's Word. It can be good to have a dress code. But when a church (or any other institution) equates its own dress code with the teaching in the Bible regarding modesty, this is the sin of legalism by addition.

People also demonstrate legalism by addition when they hold tradition above God's Word. For example, a person from a legalistic church might confront a girl they think is immodest because her shorts are four inches above the knee rather than two inches—the tradition established by that church. Even if this girl has a modest heart, the legalist can't see that; all the legalist focuses on is the girl's shorts being four inches above her knee.

To place the "two-inch" tradition of a particular church above the statements and principles from God's Word is to place tradition above Scripture. Jesus strongly denounced this form of legalism.

God never gave any literal measurements in His Word to describe what is modest or immodest. His approach must be different from the approach of the Pharisees. *To avoid legalism by addition, always keep God's Word itself separate from the specific details you use when you apply its principles.* God's Word applies to everyone and we are commanded to be doers of His Word (James 1:22–25). Not everyone, however, interprets or even applies God's Word the same way, especially when it comes to areas like modesty. God hasn't given us strict requirements for what to wear, but He has told us everything that we need to know in His Word (2 Peter 1:3–4). Therefore, strict requirements are not necessary. Never add to God's Word!

The Legalism of Subtraction

The next common error of legalism can be illustrated by the concept of subtraction. This form of legalism obeys Scripture's teaching on how to live the Christian life but subtracts the godly motivation of love. Once love has been removed, this form of legalism replaces love with other motives such as fear, duty, or pride.

First Corinthians 13:1–3 addresses this problem. The motives behind the worship and service of the Corinthian church (using spiritual gifts, giving to the poor, being willing to die for the cause of Christ) were wrong. They lacked the motive of love. When the motive of love is subtracted from our actions, we end up with "nothing" (1 Corinthians 13:2–3). Good actions minus love equal a legalism that God rejects.

What does this have to do with modesty? Legalism by subtraction could mean that we dress modestly not out of love, but out of fear because we don't want to face the consequences of immodesty. This can be seen in the young woman who desires the attention that immodesty brings. The only reason she doesn't dress immodestly is because she knows it is wrong or because her parents won't let her dress that way (and would be very upset with her if she did). She obeys because it is her duty to obey. She is motivated not by a love for God and a desire to please Him but only to keep herself out of trouble. She might also be afraid of what her dad or her pastor would say. This young woman is being legalistic in her obedience, obeying not out of love but out of fear and duty. Even though she may appear to be modest, her heart is immodest.

Mark 7:20–23 reveals that our own heart is responsible for our own sin.

> And He was saying, "That which proceeds out of the man, that is what defiles the man. For from within, out of the heart of men, proceed the evil thoughts, fornications, thefts, murders, adulteries, deeds of coveting *and* wickedness, *as well as* deceit, sensuality, envy, slander, pride *and* foolishness. All these evil things proceed from within and defile the man."

A young woman who is sensual and immodest cannot blame society, peer pressure, clothing designers, fashion styles, ignorance, or anything else. Immodesty comes from an immodest heart.

A young woman may be tempted to dress sensually until she remembers that God is her Lord and Master whom she loves. Since she wants to please Him with all her heart, she chooses not to dress immodestly. Of course she knows that God requires her obedience, and she realizes that her dad might be disappointed with her, but it is her *love* for God that is the most important motivation for her to dress and act modestly. Because of this love for God, she chooses to dress modestly and repents of her sinful heart's desire. This choice comes from a modest heart that will reveal itself in the external evidence of modesty in appearance, actions, and words.

Another trap of legalism by subtraction is to dress modestly, not because of love, but out of pride. Rather than dressing modestly in order to point people to God, this person dresses modestly to draw attention to *self*. The only difference is the motive. This is exactly the kind of attitude that Jesus strongly condemns in Matthew 6:1–18. The Pharisees gave money for the poor, they prayed, and they fasted. These are all great things for a believer to do! Jesus' problem with these Pharisees was their motive behind these actions. They gave, prayed, and fasted to impress people with how religious they were. Then they looked down upon others who didn't act as they did.

If your motive for dressing modestly is to draw attention to how modest you are (or how immodest *others* are), you are displaying the prideful legalism that Jesus strongly condemned in the Pharisees. Without the motive of love, the young woman who obeyed out of fear could easily become conceited and prideful, telling herself how upright she is and looking down on other girls who aren't as modest as she is. Remember that God alone deserves all glory, and we try to steal His glory when we draw attention to ourselves rather than point people to Him. The difference is the subtlety of motive behind the appearance of modesty.

Legalism by subtraction can be difficult to recognize in one's heart, because motives like fear, duty, and pride can be tricky to identify. The other motives of pleasing your parents and your pastor are helpful only when you remember that God is the one who said you should please them. Obedience is ultimately between you and God. He has placed others in your life as your authority, but you obey them because God said you are to obey them. Then again, don't obey God merely because it is your duty but because you love Him! It is your love for God that keeps this sinful legalism by subtraction out of your life.

Here are some questions you can ask yourself to reveal whether legalism is motivating your choices.

- Why do I want to dress this way? ("I don't know" isn't an acceptable answer. Spend some time thinking about your motives. Ask God to reveal your motives to you.)
- Is there something I am afraid of? What is it?
- Am I trying to please God with my choices?
- Am I trying to please others with my choices? If so, who am I trying to impress, and why am I trying to impress them? (Remember that it is important to consider others when making choices about what to wear and how to act. But it isn't good if legalism or pleasing people at the expense of pleasing God are the motives behind your consideration of others.)
- What do I hope will be the result of my choices?

If you find it difficult to obey out of love, I would suggest that you read just about anything that John Piper has written. The continuing refrain in many of his books is that "God is most glorified in us when we are most satisfied in Him."

What really satisfies you? Typically, we hope that we will be satisfied by that which we love. I love pizza, and I ate it almost every day in my junior and senior years of high school. The problem with pizza is that it only temporarily satisfies. I want more pizza later. The only reason I stop eating at a pizza buffet is that I get full. I still want more. Unlike pizza, if your primary satisfaction comes from your relationship with God, you will continue to be profoundly satisfied. Your love for God will grow as your relationship with Him grows, and you will experience true, complete satisfaction.

It is important to say and do things that please God (Colossians 3:17). But these words and actions are insufficient when love is not the primary motivation behind them. This legalism of subtraction will never please God!

The Legalism of Algebra

Algebra seems to hold a special hatred among math-haters. Whoever thought that numbers weren't challenging enough and decided to use letters surely succeeded in creating mass confusion. But for those who love the abstract thinking involved in algebra, enjoy the "warm fuzzies" that come from your algebraic memories as you work through this section.

Behind this legalism of algebra metaphor is the idea of *replacement*. Algebra replaces numbers with letters for a variety of purposes (and most of those reasons are actually quite good, but I'll let your math teacher get into all of that). This form of legalism, though, replaces grace with works, which is never good! Let me explain.

Some try to make up for their sin by their good works. People who think they can be saved from their sin by what they say or do are legalists, because this belief ignores the heart and our need for God's grace through the cross of Christ. Many people today falsely believe that, if they do more good than bad in this world, they are headed for heaven. Scripture is exceedingly clear that good works can never save us (Ephesians 2:8–9; Titus 3:3–7). No amount of good works will ever get anyone to heaven. According to God, "all our righteous deeds are like a filthy garment"[1] (Isaiah 64:6)! They accomplish *nothing* in terms of eternity! Dressing modestly won't earn your way to heaven. It is impossible to earn your way to heaven.

For Christians, legalism through good works can still be a problem. Maybe you chose to wear some clothes that were immodest, but you rationalized that you would do it only this one time, and only because you thought you had some really good reasons. All evening long you were self-conscious and feeling guilty, even though you tried to hide the guilt feelings behind all the fun you were having. That night, when you got home, you were convicted about your immodesty, and you decided that for the next week you would try to be ultra modest. Being modest is good! But if this decision is motivated by the thought, "When I've been extremely careful to follow God's Word, He will like me again when He sees how obedient I am,"[2] this is legalism. You are using works to try to earn God's grace—an impossibility by its very definition. Grace can never be earned as a "payment for services rendered," since it is always a gift!

Any efforts that replace God's grace with man's works will always fail to please God because they are stained with sin! Rest in the grace of God and let His promises motivate you to avoid the legalism of algebra that tries to pay for sin. Works were never meant to pay for sin, either before or after people are saved from their sin. Those who have been saved by Jesus' death on the cross will demonstrate good works as a response to God's work in their life. God created us for good works (Ephesians 2:10), but these good works will never earn His favor.

Colossian Legalism

The church at Colossae had some people in its midst who were prone to legalism. Colossians 2:16–3:4 provides helpful instructions on how to combat the error of legalism. Verse 23 shows that the sin of legalism has the *appearance* of being wise and honoring to God: "These are matters which have, to be sure, the appearance of wisdom in self-made religion and self-abasement and severe treatment of the body." It looks like legalism would be a helpful approach. It seems logical.

But it's not! These matters are "*of no value* against fleshly indulgence" (Colossians 2:23). Paul is not saying that external laws can be of some small benefit in the fight against sin. He is saying external laws have *no* benefit in fighting this fight. Immodesty, which is the manifestation of sin in the heart, cannot be fought biblically by external laws. Legalism is useless in the fight against sin. The God-given antidote to legalism is a wholehearted pursuit of the things above—God and the things that please God (Colossians 3:1–4). When the heart desires lustful attention, no amount of external rules will affect the heart. When the heart desires God, the heart will be modest, and external rules will not be needed.

The Balance between the Extremes

It is not uncommon for people who fall asleep while driving to veer off to the side of the road. When the rough texture of the shoulder wakes the person up, the panicked tendency is to over-steer the vehicle, causing the vehicle to veer out of control and land in the ditch on the opposite side of the road.

A common temptation for those who come from either a legalistic background or a licentious background (see chapter 8) is to veer to the opposite extreme. This is sometimes called the *pendulum effect*, referring to the pendulum that swings from one extreme to the opposite extreme. God's goal for us is to find the balance that lies in the middle between sinful liberty and sinful legalism.

A common tendency of the person who escapes a legalistic background is to become too free. If a young woman leaves a church that measured the length of everyone's skirt who entered the door of the church building, she might celebrate her new-found "freedoms" by dressing in ways that would have gotten her sent home.

For those who used to dress immodestly and are convicted by this sin, a common tendency is to dress modestly while pridefully judging those who have yet to learn God's will in this matter. We looked at this principle from Romans 14:1–13 in the last chapter. Examine yourself first, before you ever begin to judge others, and then proceed cautiously in humility and grace to help the person who may be struggling with immodesty.

It is vital to remember that you cannot examine the heart of another person. In fact, we are forbidden to judge heart motives in others (1 Corinthians 4:5). The only way we can accurately judge other people is to evaluate the words and deeds that they say and do (Matthew 7:16–20). Their words and deeds originate in their hearts with what they are thinking (Matthew 12:34–35). Even when we do this, our judgment is limited since we cannot see the heart as God sees it (1 Samuel 16:7). Be careful in how you judge others regarding immodesty (Matthew 7:1–6).

Conclusion

Balanced, loving obedience can come only when God is first in your life, the greatest desire of your heart. Love God! Find your satisfaction in Him rather than in the attention you can draw with immodesty. This is the key to avoiding legalism! When your heart is right, the rest of your life will follow! Is God your passion? Do you care more about what He thinks of you than about what your peers think?

It is this attitude of loving obedience, stemming from faith in Jesus, that destroys the tendencies toward legalism by addition, subtraction, and algebra. It is this attitude that we find in our Savior, Jesus Christ, "who for the joy set before Him endured the cross" (Hebrews 12:2). For the joy set before you, pursue modesty by disentangling yourself from the trappings of worldliness, no matter what it costs you!

Review Questions

1. We have freedom in the Lord to maintain an even higher standard than God requires. However, how might someone sin in spite of their outward appearance?
2. What was wrong with the Pharisees' rules and regulations?
3. Match the following:

The Pharisees saw Jesus' disciples eating with unclean hands	Proverbs 30:5-6
What Jesus said defiled a person	Colossians 2:23
God has given us everything we need to live a godly life	Mark 7:1-5
Warning about adding to God's Word	Mark 7:14
Legalism has the outward appearance of honoring God	2 Peter 1:3-4

4. What is wrong with the "legalism of subtraction"?
5. What *should* our motivation be for modesty?

PART FOUR

The Practice of Modesty

A Word from Martha and Pastor Kent

Some things in life are very slippery—banana peels, fish, ice, some kinds of hand lotion, and knowledge. Banana peels are relatively easy to avoid. Get your dad, brother, or friend to handle the fish, and you won't need to touch it. If you keep ice in your cup and buy the right kind of lotion, neither of these should be a problem. Knowledge, though, isn't quite so easy. It is so slippery that it seems to slide in one ear and right out the other. Our culture loves to let knowledge slip around in and out of our minds without letting it affect our lives. This is not God's purpose for knowledge, though. Knowledge should grip our lives so that it changes us!

Now that you have read what the Bible teaches about modesty and immodesty, what are you going to do about it? The Lord Jesus promised the apostles that He would send the Holy Spirit, who would "convict the world concerning sin" (John 16:8). Is the Holy Spirit convicting *you* of the sin of immodesty? Does what the Bible says make you angry? Remember James 1:19–20: "Be . . . slow to anger; for the anger of man does not achieve the righteousness of God." In this context, anger is most probably anger against what the Word of God teaches (James 1:18, 21). James warns us against this. Instead we are to receive the Word of God with humility. We are to plant it deep in our hearts (James 1:21) so that it takes root, grows, and bears fruit pleasing to God.

James goes on to say in 1:22–27 that those who obey God's Word will be blessed by God. Those who know what the Word says but do not apply it to their lives deceive themselves into thinking that they are spiritual when their religion is really worthless. So again we ask, what will you do about all of this?

This final section applies God's Word to this subject of immodesty with practical guidelines. The challenge is to avoid legalism on the one hand, while on the other hand to avoid the sinful expression of "supposed" liberty that actually displeases God.

Ultimately it is the role of the Holy Spirit to convict of sin (John 16:8–11). But what, then, is our responsibility? We have the responsibility to work toward holiness in our own lives. "So then, my beloved, just as you have always obeyed, not as in my presence only, but now much more in my absence, work out your salvation with fear and trembling" (Philippians 2:12). We also have a responsibility to depend on God to make us holy as we are "working out our salvation in fear and trembling." "For it is God who is at work in you, both to will and to work for His good pleasure" (Philippians 2:13). You see, God *will* do His work within us through the Holy Spirit as we also apply the truths of God's Word to our own lives!

This work toward holiness doesn't depend on individuals only. Church members also have a responsibility to confront those in their midst who don't repent of their sin (Matthew 18:15–20; Galatians 6:1–2). This is called *church discipline*, and while it's not common in our day, it is a biblical gift from God to help sinning Christians to do as they should. This act of love seeks what is best for all involved.

We urge you, if you are convicted of the sin of immodesty, to do whatever it takes to repent for your good, for the purity of the church, and, ultimately, for the glory of God! This repentance will bring you joy as the weight of a guilty conscience is removed. More importantly, repentance will restore your relationship with God so that you will "Rejoice in the Lord" (Philippians 4:4).

10

So, How Can I Be Modest?

A Word from Pastor Kent

How would you like it if someone described you simply by the color of your hair, eyes, and skin—your physical appearance—when there is obviously so much more about you? What if people took one glance at what you are wearing right now and made judgments about you that would last the rest of your life? I would hate for my significance to be based on such superficial and simplistic perspectives, especially as I grow older. (You may be young and beautiful, so the thought of being viewed in such one-dimensional ways may be appealing at the moment.) It would be a tragedy if we were all reduced to one aspect of our being.

You may remember Condoleezza Rice, the sixty-sixth United States Secretary of State and a member of President George W. Bush's cabinet. It would be a crime to take one glance at her and reduce all her accomplishments to the observation that she is a beautiful woman. Even though she is attractive, she has accomplished much in her life through her education and career. She even loves the NFL (that's football)! It wouldn't be surprising if she ran for president someday.

Most women who I know hate to be thought of only in terms of their physical appeal (at least the ones I've heard from on the subject). Such a superficial judgment is incomplete at best. Physical appeal is only one of *many* characteristics that describe each of us. Keeping all these characteristics together is important for an accurate view of who someone really is.

Unfortunately, this same error happens far too often with God's Word—and I am not referring to how beautiful the leather cover is, but to how Scripture verses are sometimes ripped from their context and applied in ways God never intended. It is so easy to pull out a few statements of the Bible and make them say what you want them to say. For example, the Bible states, "The fool has said in his heart, 'There is no God'" (Psalm 14:1). Taking that last phrase out of context, you could say, "See, even the Bible says that there is no God."

What does all of this have to do with modesty? People often try to reduce godliness to a list of principles to be followed—a checklist, if you will. Scripture checklists, however, can be harmful because they tend to be simplistic. This is like judging a person by only the outward appearance. You do not get an accurate picture. Checklists that are out of context reduce the profound truth of God's Word to a few simple statements that are easily misunderstood.

Practical guidelines for dressing modestly are also in danger of relying on biblical principles that are out of context. This results in a checklist of what to wear, say, and do, and what *not* to wear, say, and do.

My point is that if you have skipped chapters 1 through 9 and are reading this chapter because you want to know the practical "dos and don'ts," of what to wear, you will not be getting the entire picture. Please go back and read the previous chapters so that you understand the foundational issues that are involved. If you start here, you will miss the heart of modesty!

Part of the challenge in dealing with modesty is being clear about what is and is not immodest. The following list of suggestions is in no way complete. If your heart's desire is to be modest, you will find ways to glorify God as you meditate on how to pursue modesty. This list is offered in an attempt to provide some helpful thoughts that will direct you toward modesty.

1. Examine Your Motives

First of all, realize that God is the One who searches the heart and tests the mind (see Jeremiah 17:9–10). So ask God to reveal your motives behind why you want to wear the clothes you are considering. As He answers this prayer, and as you are honest with yourself, you will probably be able to evaluate whether your desires are in line with God's will or contrary to God's will.

In evaluating your motives, ask who it is that you want to impress. The apostle Paul asked himself exactly the same question in Galatians 1:10: "For am I now seeking the favor of men, or of God? Or am I striving to please men? If I were still trying to please men, I would not be a bond-servant of Christ." While the answer, of course, should be God, we often want to impress others at least on some level. When that happens, ask the all-important follow-up questions: "How am I trying to impress them?" and "Why am I trying to impress them with these choices?" Are you trying to get their attention by revealing what God wants you to cover, or are you trying to get their attention by your godly behavior, which is more easily seen with your modest styles? The more you understand your motives behind what you want to wear, the easier it will be to choose the way of modesty.

2. Honor Your Parents

Second, if you are living at home with your parents, what do they think? What, especially, does your dad think? Your mom may or may not understand the issue of immodesty and what contributes to the lust that guys struggle with, but your dad probably will. As your parents, they are worthy of being honored and obeyed simply because God says you must submit to them (Ephesians 6:1–3; Colossians 3:20). If you dishonor your parents, you are actually dishonoring God, since He commands you to honor them!

Another reason to honor your parents is because of what Solomon told his son. Solomon told him that he would lack the guidance he would need in the future if he dishonored his parents (Proverbs 20:20). The New Testament provides other principles to motivate you to honor your parents: because it is right (Ephesians 6:1), so that it will go well with you (Ephesians 6:3), so that you will live a long time (Ephesians 6:3), and so that you will please the Lord (Colossians 3:20).

Do you listen to what your parents have to say about how you act, speak, and dress? Are you honoring them? Honoring goes way beyond simple obedience. You can perfectly obey your parents externally but still dishonor them by complaining in your heart toward them.

The story is told about the three-year-old who refused to sit down when her parents told her to sit down. Finally she sat down but proudly proclaimed, "I'm sitting down on the outside, but inside I'm still standing up!" While this may sound cute (especially since you are not her parents), it isn't right! Honor obeys externally *and* internally in our actions and our thoughts.

Do you hate to go shopping with your parents because they never let you buy clothes that you think are fine but they think are immodest? Do you hide certain clothes from your parents by wearing bulky sweatshirts or jackets and then wear what you want when you get to school? Do you try to sneak out of the house without letting them see what you're wearing for the day? If you feel the need to hide your clothing from your parents, you are not honoring them.

This issue of immodesty and lust can be quite confusing.

Even if you don't understand or don't agree with your parents' concern, trust them. If they are willing to help you in your pursuit of modesty, accept their help, even if you think they are being too conservative in their sense of fashion and style. If you don't understand, ask them to share their valuable insights into the confusing male species.

Your parents have a serious responsibility for your life, and they will someday give an account for it in the presence of God. Because of that, you may want to have your parents read the appendix at the end of this book, which shows how they can help you to be modest, if they are willing. It is a letter for them from us.

There is one last principle that hopefully does not apply to many people—but, if it describes your situation, please understand God's will in this matter. If you have the desire to be modest but your parents are urging you to dress or behave immodestly, for whatever reason, understand that you must obey God rather than your parents.

No one, not even your pastors, your teachers, police, government officials, or even your parents, has the authority to contradict anything that God requires. The apostles experienced this in Acts 4–5 when the Jewish religious leaders arrested the apostles to stop them from preaching about Jesus, which He Himself required (Matthew 28:18–20). The apostles honored Jesus' authority by not obeying the Jewish authorities who were trying to usurp God's authority. The apostles answered, "We must obey God rather than men" (Acts 5:29; see also Acts 4:19–20).

Likely this will never happen to you, but if it does, consider the following verses:

> No temptation has overtaken you but such as is common
> to man; and God is faithful, who will not allow you to be
> tempted beyond what you are able, but with the temptation

will provide the way of escape also, that you may be able to endure it. (1 Corinthians 10:13)

And He has said to me, "My grace is sufficient for you, for power is perfected in weakness." Most gladly, therefore, I will rather boast about my weaknesses, so that the power of Christ may dwell in me. (2 Corinthians 12:9)

As God's grace *was* sufficient for the apostle Paul, so God's grace *will* be sufficient for you in every trial you face as a believer. Trust Him as you endure these challenges. You may also want to ask one of the leaders in your church to help you if you have earthly authorities demanding that you sin.

A Word from Martha

3. Study Your Mirror

Next, ask your mirror to show you possible ways that you may be immodest. "Mirror, mirror on the wall, who's the most modest girl in the mall?" Or at school? Or at church? Actually, modesty isn't a matter of comparing yourself to others, but to God's standard for modesty. The goal is not to spend too much time looking at yourself in the mirror, but rather to examine your appearance from many angles so that you are modest from any perspective.

There are many things to check in the mirror:

Are your clothes too tight? You may not be exposing bare skin, but are your clothes so tight that nakedness is only a technicality? If your outer clothes are simply another layer of skin, you are being immodest. Check your blood pressure to see if you are cutting off your blood supply with those tight clothes. Are any parts turning blue? OK, not seriously, but you get the point. Some clothes are too tight.

How tight is too tight? Wrong question! The right perspective asks, "Are these clothes loose enough to cover those parts of my body that should be kept private?" Especially check garments with a lot of latex in them—though latex garments may not necessarily be immodest. It's helpful to ask, though, why you need your clothes to stretch if they should be loose. If you are about to pop some buttons off your blouse, move up to the next size, or else you'll be offering glimpses of what ought not to be glimpsed.

Is your neckline too low? Bend over, lift your head up, and see what you are showing to others when you pick something up from the floor. You might have to layer your clothing to end up with a modest neckline. Make sure your cleavage is *completely* covered so that no hint of immodesty is given to others.

Is your shirt or blouse too high at the waist? Are your shorts, pants, or skirt too low on your waist? When your hands are raised over your head, is your shirt low enough? Is your skirt so short that you have to be careful how you sit down and get up? Are your shorts drawing attention to what they cover? In fact, ask yourself, "Where does this style or piece of clothing (whatever it is) focus attention?" You may be covering your private parts, but if your clothes are designed to focus the attention of others upon those parts, then don't wear them. Writing, fade lines, and other decorative means are often a way to draw attention to certain parts of the body.

Are you exposing parts of the body that are sensually suggestive? Pastor Kent remembers visiting a church for the first time and seeing, in the second row, a woman wearing a top that apparently covered the front of her body, but the only bit of clothing showing to those sitting behind her was a thin piece to tie from each side. Her entire back was exposed. The back may not be considered a "private part," but it is normally seen only when one is naked. The power of suggestion can be as immodest as being completely uncovered.

Do your undergarments show through? It is best if guys get no hint of what style of underwear you have chosen to wear, whether it is visible through other material or because parts of your undergarments have become outer garments. Even a glimpse of a strap can get the imagination going. In my grandmother's day, undergarments were called "unmentionables." We have gone way past the stage where we don't even speak of undergarments. Publicly displaying undergarments has, sadly, become the fashion. A recent style of jeans rides so low on the hips that the edges of undergarments are clearly seen. This helps no one!

Are you constantly aware of the potential for immodesty in what you are wearing? Are you constantly adjusting your clothes? Sometimes it seems rather obvious that teens are feeling a little guilty about what they wear. They are so aware of being potentially immodest that they are always adjusting their clothes, rearranging how they sit, and simply looking uncomfortable. If you find yourself in such a situation, then get out of it as quickly as possible and take whatever steps are necessary so that it does not repeat itself.

What does the slogan on your T-shirt say? Is this something that godly people would say? Also, you don't need to wear shorts that have writing across the back. In addition, be careful of wearing T-shirts with slogans across your chest. The same principle applies to suggestive tattoos and body piercings. The purpose of these words, images, and jewelry is to draw attention to those parts of your body that guys should not be thinking about! These parts are to be concealed. Be careful of how and what you are advertising.

Do you dress like "one of the guys"? Deuteronomy 22:5 says, "A woman shall not wear man's clothing, nor shall a man put on a woman's clothing; for whoever does these things is an abomination to the LORD your God."

Why this command? One possible reason is that cross-dressing may reflect discontentment with the gender that God has made you to be. While men and women are equal beings in the eyes of God (Galatians 3:28; 1 Peter 3:7), He consistently separates males and females in both roles and appearance (1 Corinthians 11:2–16). God is the one who knit us together in our mothers' wombs to be the gender that we are (Psalm 139:13–16). Any resistance to being content with the gender that God made us is ultimately rebellion against God Himself.

The word that Deuteronomy uses in this passage is "abomination." Deuteronomy 22:5 shows that God hates it when men dress like women and when women dress like men. In my understanding, this means that people should be able to determine your gender at a glance.

One way that the principle of Deuteronomy 22:5 can be applied is to those young women who are "tomboys." I am not against girls participating in athletics or spending appropriate time with guys, but this needs to be done as a girl—not as "one of the guys."

God doesn't make any mistakes! He made you the way you are so that even your gender will bring Him glory. If you are discontented about being a woman and try to dress and act like a man instead, then you are dishonoring God by thinking that He made a mistake about you. Modesty includes joyful submission to God's plan for your life, including your gender.

Why do you wear the makeup that you do? There is a place for makeup—in the appropriate amount and colors. Makeup can have a downside, however. Hayley DiMarco states her concern this way:

> Just like your clothes, your makeup reveals to guys what kind of a girl you are. And the truth is, the more makeup, the more sex the guy thinks he's going to get, or at least the more he'll fantasize about. . . . A girl with thick black eyeliner and bright red lips speaks volumes to everyone around her. Guys are thinking, *She's ready for anything.* She's got a sign out in front of the shop, saying "open for business and accepting new clients." Tons of makeup is an invitation to guys of all ages to come onto you. Whereas a little less makeup, let's say, the natural look, can just give you an allover healthy glow without screaming "older and more experienced."[1]

This gives you another insight into how a guy thinks. Remember how we talked about being careful how we fish for attention? Well, the more makeup you wear, the more likely you are to attract the wrong kind of attention!

Before we leave this third point, there are two helpful checklists that I want to recommend. One list is found in the book *Girl Talk*.[2] At the time of writing, this same checklist can also be found at the Sovereign Grace Ministries website.[3] Another helpful list is found in the book *Every Young Woman's Battle*.[4]

You can also choose to use your mirror in a little mental role-playing. As you stand in front of the mirror, pretend that you are standing in front of your church congregation! (It is scary to stand in front of all those people with their eyes all focused on you alone, isn't it?) What you see in the mirror is what they would see. How would these people who worship God with you think about the way in which you are dressed? (We're not talking about whether the orange blouse would go with the pink skirt. We're talking about modesty versus immodesty!)

Would there be any who would disapprove with good reasons? Think of your pastor, your church leaders, any elderly women in your congregation, the little girls who look up to you, as well as all the guys who might be struggling to control their thought lives. Is the way that you want to dress helpful to all these people, or would some have problems with how you dress?

Your mirror can be a great friend and ally in your fight against personal immodesty. If you like what you see in your friend, the mirror, thank God for this with humility.

4. Be Consistently Modest

Finally, resolve not to make exceptions for exceptional situations. Jeff Pollard, in his booklet *Christian Modesty and the Public Undressing of America*, reveals how the swimsuit industry has intentionally and systematically lowered the standards of modesty.[5] Do you allow yourself to be immodest when you go to the beach just because everyone else is immodest at the beach? The beach (or the swimming pool) is not a "no-application zone" for the Word of God. What God has said in His Word applies to everyone, everywhere, always!

Summer in general is the time to be especially concerned about immodesty (unless you live in a tropical climate, in which case the concern is year around). Melody Green understands this! She writes,

> In the summertime especially, we have our biggest opportunity to test our consecration to Jesus. Sheer blouses, halter tops, "short" shorts, and skimpy bathing-suits are the norm for many careless Christian women. They use the rationalization that "it's hot" or "I'm swimming" to excuse their lack of modesty. Clothes that fit too tightly, tops that are cut too low, and skirts that are cut too short are not only a distraction to those around us—but the wearers show an unloving lack of concern for their responsibility as a representative of Jesus. Unfortunately, it seems that many Christians are lost in their own selfish little world—either oblivious or uncaring about the effect they have on others.[6]

Pastor Kent was speaking with the mother of a teenager who shared how much of a challenge it was to find a modest dress for the formal event her daughter was attending. They were unable to find a dress that wasn't cut too low in front and especially in the back, or one whose straps were appropriate and not suggestive. Her solution was to buy two dresses and then pay a seamstress to sew a modest jacket from the second dress to go with the first dress. What commitment to our God! The cost was much more than it would cost to be immodest, but such decisions honor our glorious God! That is money well spent.

Do you have to be selective when you show your prom pictures? Did you feel self-conscious about all the skin you were baring when you wore that dress to the formal you attended? Weddings are joyous occasions that shouldn't be marred by immodesty. The Albert Mohler Radio Program has dealt with this specific topic. The show's title asked the question, "Are Christian Women 'Modeling Modesty' in Weddings?"[7] No matter who you are at the wedding—a guest, a bridesmaid, or especially the bride—don't let your standards slip into sinfulness.

Don't allow yourself to dress immodestly "just this once." There is no occasion that is special enough to justify the sin of immodesty. Just because you fit into the style of the event and you are "relatively modest" does not mean that you are pleasing God. In this case, relative modesty is just another term for immodesty! Establish biblical, God-pleasing standards, and choose to hold to them no matter what!

Another Word from Pastor Kent

Suggestions for the Fight against Immodesty

If you find that you have clothes that are immodest, then you need to get rid of them. If you are afraid that you will have nothing left to wear, then go buy some new clothes. You may love the fit of the clothes you need to get rid of. You may have many wonderful memories attached to them, but a love for God means that you please Him and not yourself.

It is hard work developing biblical convictions about modesty in our culture today. Once you have these convictions, unfortunately, your work isn't over. Now you need a store where you can find modest clothing. This will probably take more time and even more money, since the majority of those in our culture are not committed to modesty. You may want to ask a modest friend where she shops. There seems to be a growing trend for some places to offer modest clothing as a reaction to our culture. The Internet can help you to find these places. Even though modesty is more costly and time consuming, pleasing God is definitely worth it!

While concluding my research for this book, I came across a

helpful sermon from John Barnett that summarizes much of this book. I suggest that you take the time to look up the Scripture references as you read through this list. Pastor Barnett shows how we can meet our goal of having modest behavior from a modest heart by keeping the following in mind:

- God invented clothing to cover us (Genesis 3:21).
- Clothes can be beautiful (Proverbs 31:22), or they can be enticing (Proverbs 7:10).
- God's design for clothing is to clearly mark us as men and women (Deuteronomy 22:5) and to prevent lust, not encourage it (1 Timothy 2:9; 2 Peter 2:14).
- Clothing should help us to *avoid* sinful, manipulative behavior that leads to eternal consequences (Proverbs 7:13–14, 21–23; Galatians 6:7–8; 1 Peter 3:4).
- We should dress as those who are separate from the world (Deuteronomy 18:9; Jeremiah 10:2; Romans 12:2; 2 Corinthians 6:17–7:1).
- Our clothing should show our humility (Isaiah 3:16–24; 1 Peter 5:5) instead of drawing attention to ourselves (Luke 20:46).
- Internal holiness and worth as a person comes before the external appearance (James 2:1–2; 1 Peter 3:3–5).
- Ultimately, we should "put on" Christ (Romans 13:13–14).[8]

I hope you find this helpful as you desire to please God with your modesty. Remember, more than anything else, modesty *begins* in the heart and then expresses itself through your words, actions, and dress. If you want to be modest, it will help if you examine your motives, honor your parents, study your mirror, and be consistently modest! After all, modesty is more than just a change of clothes.

Review Questions

1. Ask yourself, "Are my desires for how I dress in line with God's will for me? Am I honoring my parents by being modest?"

2. According to Ephesians 6:1–3 and Colossians 3:20, why *should* you honor your parents by how you act, speak, and dress?

3. What should you do and say in the very unlikely event that your parents want you to dress immodestly? Use Scripture to explain your answer.

4. Why is dressing and acting like a boy wrong if you are a girl?

5. Tomorrow morning, after you dress and put on makeup, stand in front of the mirror and look at yourself. What do *you* see? What will *others* see? What does *God* see?

6. Just before the end of this chapter, there is a bulleted list that summarizes much of this book. Read over the list again. Look up the Scriptures and think about them. Ask yourself, "Am I *really* pleasing to God in this area of my life?"

11

What Should I Do about This?

A Word from Martha

Pastor Kent is going to explain how to pursue modesty. But, first, I want to tell you something that the apostle Peter wrote. It's what was on his mind shortly before he was martyred for the Lord. Peter had several outstanding qualities, but one particularly stands out in my mind—he was enthusiastic. Right or wrong, he jumped right in and spoke his mind. Of course, when he was wrong, it got him into a lot of trouble.

In Peter's enthusiasm, he wanted to protect the Lord. In fact, he was willing to give his life to protect Jesus, and there were times when Peter boldly proclaimed what he would do. Sadly, though, after Jesus had been arrested and a little servant-girl pointed out that Peter was one of the disciples, Peter panicked and denied the Lord. In spite of that colossal failure, Jesus forgave him and used Peter greatly for His glory.

After Jesus' resurrection, Peter boldly preached on the day of Pentecost. Thousands heard him and he ended his sermon with the following words: "Therefore let all the house of Israel know *for certain* that God has made Him both Lord and Christ—this Jesus whom you crucified" (Acts 2:36). Peter was sure, and, as far as we know, he never doubted or denied the Lord again. He knew that openly preaching the gospel meant that he was risking his life. Eventually he was martyred for the Lord.

Not only did Peter preach at Pentecost, but he was a leader of the church in Jerusalem. Later on, he wrote the books of 1 and 2 Peter, and he greatly influenced Mark when Mark wrote his gospel. One of the things on Peter's mind when he wrote his last two letters (1 and 2 Peter) was that *true* Christians continue to grow and mature in the Christian faith. In 2 Peter 1:6, he wrote that true Christians will be maturing in several areas of their lives, one of which is knowledge: knowledge of God's character, knowledge of the Lord Jesus, and knowledge of how to grow as a Christian by God's grace.

Because knowledge is so important, the following warning and command was the last thing that Peter wrote:

> You therefore, beloved, knowing this beforehand, be on your guard lest, being carried away by the error of unprincipled men, you fall from your own steadfastness, but *grow in the grace and knowledge of our Lord and Savior Jesus Christ.* To Him be the glory, both now and to the day of eternity. Amen. (2 Peter 3:17–18)

Making effort to grow in God's grace and in knowledge is a lifelong process. It is one of the ways that we pursue godliness in our lives, and, of course, that includes modesty. Pastor Kent is going to tell you how.

A Word from Pastor Kent

I love chocolate, especially the rich European kinds. Normally after lunch I'll eat a little bit of chocolate. Sometimes I get distracted and forget about my after-lunch treat. Or sometimes I put it off because I plan on having a special dessert later that day. My wife normally keeps some kind of chocolate at home for me, and I try to keep some in my desk at the office. I've made arrangements in my life to enjoy this blessing from God, usually in moderation. We tend to make arrangements to enjoy anything that we really want.

It is the same with modesty. If you want to be modest, you will arrange your life so that you are modest inside and out. The only question is this: do you want to be modest enough so that you are willing to do all that is required to be modest?

Pursue Modesty by Repenting of Immodesty

If you are convicted of immodesty, then repent. Repentance is accepting the blame for your sin and not excusing it. Jessica Rabbit, the seductive woman in the movie *Who Framed Roger Rabbit*, says, "I'm not bad; I'm just drawn that way."[1] You don't have this excuse, since you were created by God to present your beauty modestly. You cannot blame anyone else.

Repentance means doing whatever it takes to please God and not continue in this sin or even make provision for this sin (Romans 13:14). If you know you have sinned against your parents, your boyfriend, or others, confess your sin to God and those you sinned against, and ask their forgiveness. If you still have immodest clothing, throw it out.

Pursue Modesty through a Growing Relationship with God

More than anything else, you will find your greatest help in modesty by developing a passion to grow in your relationship with God. Study the Bible to see His character. Spend time meditating on how His character should affect how you live. Grow a tender, biblically trained conscience, and listen to it. A clear conscience is a precious gift that will draw you close to God. When your conscience tells you that you have sinned—and we all sin quite often—confess it quickly and do anything necessary to honor God in repenting from that sin. Guilt—what you experience when you ignore your conscience and refuse to repent—creates the desire to hide from God. Ultimately, guilt ignored will sear your conscience so that it will stop convicting you of sin.

If God is your greatest delight, the temptations of this world will not be able to entice you into their sinful web. You will see them for what they are—artificial lures that promise satisfaction but are really only a sharp hook designed to drag you as far away from God as possible. God wants something far better for you. He wants to satisfy your every desire as you follow His ways (Psalm 37:4; Ecclesiastes 11:9)! Only God's ways truly satisfy.

As C. J. Mahaney has written, "Reflect on the wonder of the cross of Christ." He continues by quoting John Owen: "Fill your affections with the cross of Christ . . . that there may be no room for sin."[2]

Pursue Modesty by Avoiding the Influences of the World

Also, be careful of who you allow to influence you. A faithful servant of God who I served with in junior high ministry attributes some of today's problems with immodesty to the old TV show *Friends*. The actresses wore tight shirts with low necklines, and it became popular to dress in that way. Shows like these are not your friends, as they glorify what God says is immoral.

There is no doubt that what goes into our hearts influences us profoundly. In fact, Proverbs 4:23 warns us to "Watch over your heart with all diligence." What influences do you allow to have an effect upon your life? Do you buy all the magazines, trying to learn the latest tips on what to wear and how to get the attention of the guy you dream about? Do you submit yourself to the mind-controlling attempts of the media, whose goal is to get you to think the way it wants you to think? Are you taking fashion notes from the TV? What about the Internet?

Pursue Modesty by Developing Wise Friendships

I believe there is a stronger influence than the various types of media: our friends. There are few relationships that are more important to teens than friends. Tears often accompany friendlessness. Broken friendships and relationships frequently contribute to attempts at suicide. Friendships have a powerful pull upon us.

God knows this. He provided guidelines in His Word for this! Such an important part of life must be evaluated in light of what the Bible says about friendships. The book of Proverbs has much to say about friendship. It helps us to know the kinds of friends that we *should* allow to influence us (3:32; 13:20; 17:17; 18:24). Proverbs also describes twelve characteristics that we should be sure are absent from those who become our friends and who may influence us. The chart on the next page describes these characteristics, the command from God to avoid people who have them, and the consequence you will typically experience if you disobey God in this.

These are devastating consequences! Notice especially how many horrible consequences come from seduction (sexual immorality). More than anything else, unwise romantic relationships have been the instrument that has pulled students, ones who had previously been a faithful part of our ministry, away from the things of God. The desire to have that "special someone" has led to their willingness to compromise convictions that honor God. This desire, for those enslaved by this sin, becomes an idol!

I encourage students who have problems in choosing wise friends to go through this list and ask themselves two questions. What do the characteristics of the wrong kind of friends look like? Do you have any close friends with these characteristics?

THE WRONG KINDS OF FRIENDS

	Characteristics of Wrong Kinds of Friends	Commands from God	Consequences in Your Life
1.	Violent 1:11–19; 3:31; 16:29	Do not walk with them Keep your feet from their path Do not choose any of their ways	Ambushing your own life Taking life away Being led in an evil way
2.	Perverse (immoral) 2:11–16	(No commands in this text)	Darkness, evil, perversity
3.	Seductive 2:16–19; 5:1–14; 6:20–35; 7:1–27; 29:3	Keep away from them Don't desire their beauty Restrain your heart Avoid	Death, not returning from her trap, divorce, cruelty, losing your rewards, illnesses, regret, ruin, being consumed, being burnt by sin, punishment, destruction, disgrace, reproach, slaughter, being entrapped, wasting wealth
4.	Foolish 13:20; 14:7; 17:12	Leave the presence of a fool	Harm Not discerning knowledge Being better to meet a momma bear whose cubs have been stolen
5.	Gossiping 20:19	Do not associate with them	Secrets being revealed
6.	Scoffing 22:10	Drive out the scoffer	Contention, strife, dishonor
7.	Angry 22:24–25	Do not associate with them Do not go with them	Learning his ways, being ensnared
8.	Drunken 23:20–21	Do not be with them	Poverty
9.	Gluttonous 23:20–21; 28:7	Do not be with them	Poverty Humiliating your father
10.	Evil 24:1–2	Do not envy them, nor desire to be with them	Violence and trouble
11.	Fickle Undependable 24:21–22	Do not associate with them	Sudden, unknown calamity
12.	Stealing 29:24	(No commands in this text)	Hating your own life

For example, the characteristic "fickle" might describe a person who one day is a close friend but, the next day when something trivial happens, is no longer your friend. Then, the following day, the friendship is back in place. This kind of person knows very little about loyalty and faithfulness in friendships. You should not allow a person with this characteristic to be one of your close friends who has an influence upon your life. If this fickle "friend" encourages you toward fickleness, you are too close and need to put some distance between you both so that her sin doesn't become your sin.

There are other strong warnings against foolish friendships. Psalm 1:1 tells us, "How blessed is the man who does not walk in the counsel of the wicked, nor stand in the path of sinners, nor sit in the seat of scoffers!" The apostle Paul was clear when he wrote "not to associate with any so-called brother if he should be an immoral person, or covetous, or an idolater, or a reviler, or a drunkard, or a swindler—not even to eat with such a one" (1 Corinthians 5:11). There are few decisions in life that are more important than who you allow to influence your life through friendship. Be careful what and who you allow to influence your life. Godly friends will encourage you to please God. Worldly friends tend to hate your desire to please God. Don't allow people who are characterized by sinfulness to influence you toward sin.

It is very important to have a different kind of relationship than this with unbelievers and professing believers who sin and don't repent (1 Corinthians 5:11). God's Word teaches that Christians are to have an influence upon others (Matthew 5:13–16). In fact, God put us in this world not to be a part of it (see John 17), but to be His ambassador of reconciliation to it (2 Corinthians 5:20–21). We do this by being Christians who encourage others to glorify God by how we live and by "speaking the truth in love" (Ephesians 4:15; see also Colossians 4:2–6; 1 Peter 3:15). Ephesians

5:11 states not only that you are *not* to be influenced by sin, but that you are to *expose* the sinfulness of others for what it is. This requires biblical wisdom, grace, and humility (Matthew 7:1–6; Galatians 6:1–2).

Create a group of friends that has positive peer pressure. Find others who are like-minded, or teach others (humbly and graciously) to become like-minded. Help them to know what God thinks about modesty. Hebrews 3:13 encourages these kinds of relationships. "But encourage one another day after day, as long as it is still called 'Today,' lest any one of you be hardened by the deceitfulness of sin." We need others every day to help us in walking with God. Dare, as a group, to be uniquely modest and to live out the love of God in your lives together!

Pursue Modesty through a Courageous Delight in God

Be courageous (Joshua 1:6–8)! Dare to stand for God before the world. Be willing to stand alone for the glory of God if need be. If possible, though, surround yourself with others who desire to please God through modesty. This will be of immense help in your pursuit of a modest heart and clothing style! If you are persecuted, rejoice (Matthew 5:10–12). Don't invite persecution through foolishness, but show the difference that God's grace has made in your life.

Have you ever wondered why some people seem to be used in extraordinary ways to change the world (Acts 17:6)? I believe that it might be because of the truth we read in 2 Chronicles 16:9, which says, "For the eyes of the LORD move to and fro throughout the earth that He may strongly support those whose heart is completely His." If you have been saved from your sin and are pursuing God with all your heart, put on your seat belt and watch out! With God supporting you, you have the opportunity to turn your part of the world upside down for Christ.

Modesty is only one of many issues in life that is required for your heart to be completely God's. It can be a powerful issue, though. (Immodesty can also be quite powerful when it is wielded by our own fleshly desires.) A modest life that is supported by God will have a profound influence for His glory on those around you. That kind of power does not come easily, but those who depend on His grace will experience it as they pursue godliness!

If we could only spend five seconds in the presence of God in heaven or experience His unbridled wrath in hell, we would understand what is at stake. If we could hear the testimony of the martyrs, who throughout the last two thousand years have stood for Christ even though it cost them everything they possessed, we would understand that godliness is worth so much more than everything this world has to offer.

God gave us His Word. It is all we need to please Him (Luke 16:29–31; 2 Peter 1:3–4). He makes this demand: "But among you there must not be even a hint of sexual immorality, or of any kind of impurity, or of greed, because these are improper for God's holy people" (Ephesians 5:3 NIV).

Will you obey Him in love?

Review Questions

1. What is Peter's warning and command to Christians in 2 Peter 3:17–18?
2. What are some practical ways you can grow in your relationship with God?
3. Make a list of worldly influences that would tempt someone to be immodest. Which ones tempt you? See Proverbs 4:23.
4. From Proverbs 3:32; 13:20; 17:17; 18:24, make a list of the kinds of friends you *should* have.

5. Reread the characteristics in the chart of "The Wrong Kinds of Friends." Look up each Scripture reference and think about the *commands* from God and the *consequences* associated with them.

6. Christian friends help each other to become as much like the Lord Jesus as possible. What does Hebrews 3:13 tell us about our relationship with others?

7. What does repentance mean? What is your prayer?

12

What Hope Is There for the Immodest?

A Word from Martha

At the beginning of this book, I told you that the Lord saved me when I was thirty-three years old. Now I am more than double that! I am old enough to be your grandmother. In fact, for some of you, I *am* your grandmother! These years have been an amazing journey in God's grace. Looking back on all of them, I could not write a book long enough to tell you about all the kindnesses God has brought into my life.

My thirty-six–year journey in God's grace began the day that God saved me when He cleansed me from my sin, gave me a new heart to love and worship Him, and gave me a great desire to please Him. I was reading the gospel of John the night that God saved me. I had started at the beginning, and when I got to the fourteenth chapter, this is what the Lord Jesus said:

> Whatever you ask in My name, that will I do, that the Father
> may be glorified in the Son. . . . If you love Me, you will keep
> My commandments. (John 14:13, 15)

It was during those moments of time, as I read those words, that God made His Word real and true to me. He convicted me of my sin, and I had great sorrow over the things I had done. He also convicted me of having never ever, one time, given God glory in my entire life. I began to pray and ask forgiveness for specific sins. (It took a long time.) Then I asked Him to use my life for His glory, whatever that would mean for me.

God has answered that prayer in my life. It has been the greatest gift I have ever received and will ever receive. It is His greatest kindness to me, even though I did not deserve it.

Pastor Kent has saved the most important kindness for this last chapter. Please prayerfully read what he has written to you and think about what he is saying as you go through each paragraph. I am praying for you that you will, like I did so long ago, believe God's Word, believe the gospel, and bow yourself before God and ask Him to use you for His glory.

A Word from Pastor Kent

Assumptions are those things that often get me into trouble. If I assume that people will follow the rules of the road when driving, then I will be tempted to get upset with people who don't. If I assume that people will naturally want to be my friends, I can become disillusioned when they want nothing to do with me. If I assume that I am saving money by buying things on sale, I could end up paying more for those items whose price was raised before the "sale." Assumptions are a necessary part of life, however. Wisdom knows when to assume certain things and when not to assume them.

Wise or not, my basic assumption is that those who read this book are Christians who want to follow God's will as revealed in His Word, the Bible. My greatest desire is for you to know the Lord Jesus Christ in such a way that He becomes your greatest desire. I hope you understand that He is your Lord and Master and that you are His servant to do His will only!

Many churches today offer a false assurance of salvation that is based on some past event in your life rather than on the fruit of your life right now. The Bible measures salvation by present fruit rather than by a past event. If you believe that you are a Christian already, let me encourage you to follow two more passages of Scripture. First, 2 Corinthians 13:5 is a command to "Test yourselves to see if you are in the faith; examine yourselves! Or do you not recognize this about yourselves, that Jesus Christ is in you—unless indeed you fail the test?" Second, this is echoed by the apostle Peter in 2 Peter 1:10–11.

> Therefore, brethren, be all the more diligent to make certain about His calling and choosing you; for as long as you practice these things, you will never stumble; for in this way the entrance into the eternal kingdom of our Lord and Savior Jesus Christ will be abundantly supplied to you.

Why is this so important? Because of the scariest words in Scripture for those who believe they are saved from their sin (Matthew 7:21–23):

> Not everyone who says to Me, "Lord, Lord," will enter the kingdom of heaven; but he who does the will of My Father who is in heaven. *Many* will say to Me on that day, "Lord, Lord, did we not prophesy in Your name, and in Your name cast out demons, and in Your name perform many miracles?" And then I will declare to them, *"I never knew you; depart from Me, you who practice lawlessness."*

Notice that *many* people will be saying this to Jesus when they stand before Him in judgment. The people in this passage relied upon their experiences for the assurance of salvation they felt (prophesy, exorcism, performing miracles—for us today it might be praying the sinner's prayer, attending church, or simply being born into a Christian home). Obviously there is nothing wrong with these experiences, and God often uses these experiences for great good. But the biblical measurement for the assurance of salvation is what is happening in your life now, not what happened at some time in your past. Unfortunately, these past experiences deceive some people into thinking they are saved when they really are not.

I cannot imagine what it would be like to think I was saved, only to show up on judgment day and hear these words from Jesus: "I never knew you; depart from Me." There would be no second chance. After dreaming of heaven, to have to experience hell for all of eternity is terrible, beyond my ability to understand.

Therefore, test yourself! Make sure that what you hope and profess to be true is *actually* true. Thankfully, God has given us many places in Scripture that we can use to test our lives. The Sermon on the Mount (Matthew 5–7) shows us how believers, who are now citizens of God's kingdom, can be citizens that please Him. First John was written so that you may test yourself to know that you are saved (see 1 John 5:13). James is a great book to show what a difference true saving faith will make in a believer's life. Study these texts and many others so that you won't be surprised on the day of judgment when you stand before Jesus to give an account for the way you have lived your life (2 Corinthians 5:1–11).

Then there are those who know they are *not* saved and don't want to repent. We are all born this way and, apart from God's grace, will continue this way. Thankfully there is hope for this group, too. If you are part of this group, please do not be offended by the statements found in the rest of this chapter. These truths are not intended as disrespect for you or for anyone else. It is only because so much depends on how you respond to the gospel that I speak the way I do, out of care and concern for you.

The gospel was given for those who need to be saved. I want

to explain the gospel so that you can know, based upon the truth of the Bible, how to have eternal life.

What Is the Gospel?

Mark begins his account of Jesus' life here on earth this way: "The beginning of the gospel of Jesus Christ, the Son of God" (Mark 1:1). Jesus' first sermon in Mark calls people to "repent and believe in the gospel" (Mark 1:14–15). One hundred and eighteen times Scripture uses the Greek word that we often translate as "gospel."[1] So, what is this gospel?

We need to know exactly what the gospel is, because the consequences are way too high to be careless with it. Galatians 1:6–10 makes it clear that we must believe the *right* gospel. If anyone teaches a different gospel from that of the Bible, even if it is an angel from heaven, then that teacher of the false gospel and those who believe it are headed for hell.

Also, it is not enough to *know* exactly what the gospel is according to God as revealed in His Word. It is essential that we *respond* to it in a way that pleases God. Any other gospel or any improper response to the gospel leads straight to hell for eternity!

The Short Answer to "What Is the Gospel?"

First Corinthians 15:1–8 is a good place to start in defining what the gospel is, because this is Paul's summary of the gospel. When the Bible says in essence, "This is the gospel," it's probably a good idea to start there.

Paul begins by reminding the Corinthians what he had already taught them. It is this gospel that God used to save the Christians in Corinth (and everywhere else). It is this same gospel that God used to make the Corinthians holy as they held tightly to these truths. In 1 Corinthians 15:3, Paul says that the gospel is the most important truth in life ("first importance") and then tells us what the gospel is. See if you can find it as you read this passage.

> Now I make known to you, brethren, the gospel which I preached to you, which also you received, in which also you stand, by which also you are saved, if you hold fast the word which I preached to you, unless you believed in vain. For I delivered to you as of first importance what I also received, that Christ died for our sins according to the Scriptures, and that He was buried, and that He was raised on the third day according to the Scriptures, and that He appeared to Cephas, then to the twelve. After that He appeared to more than five hundred brethren at one time, most of whom remain until now, but some have fallen asleep; then He appeared to James, then to all the apostles; and last of all, as it were to one untimely born, He appeared to me also. (1 Corinthians 15:1–8)

Paul gives four primary elements of the "gospel of Jesus Christ, the Son of God." Did you find them? They are all focused upon Jesus. Paul tells us that Jesus:

- *Died.* He actually died. He did not faint or become unconscious. The Bible foretold that Jesus would die (Isaiah 53:4–12). Jesus Himself prophesied of these things to the apostles (Mark 8:31; 9:31; 10:33–34). His death fulfilled these prophecies!
- *Was Buried.* This gives proof that He actually died.
- *Was Raised.* The resurrection was also foretold. The apostles were told repeatedly before the death of Jesus that He would rise again, but they didn't understand this until after the resurrection! Romans 4:25 shows

that the resurrection is the reason for our salvation. God accepted the offering of Jesus upon the cross for our sin and therefore exalted Jesus, beginning with raising Him from the dead.

- *Appeared.* The many appearances of Jesus after the resurrection prove that Jesus actually returned to life. There were hundreds of eyewitnesses to this fact. We have records from four eyewitness accounts recorded in the Gospels (Matthew, Mark, Luke, and John) and another in Paul's writings (Acts 22:3–21).

To be a Christian, you must believe that these four elements literally happened to Jesus Christ, the Son of God. There can be no salvation apart from this gospel truth (John 14:6; Acts 4:12).

This is not the whole story, though, any more than the stories of Jesus' birth in the New Testament are the whole gospel. Someone can believe these facts and still not be saved. These elements are essential to the gospel, but more must be understood.

A Longer Answer to "What Is the Gospel?"

More could be said (and probably should be) than what you find here, but this is a summary of the gospel as I understand God's Word. It can be broken down into four basic sections: who God is, who man is, who Christ is, and what God demands.[2]

Who God Is. Before any other aspect of the gospel can make sense, you must have an accurate understanding of who God is. If you have a wrong view of who God is, nothing else in the gospel will be biblical or make sense. This was the problem described in Acts 17. The people were sincere and diligent in worshiping their gods, but they had it all wrong. The apostle Paul understood their need and preached the gospel to them. His clear emphasis was the character of God—who God is. To summarize Acts 17:22–31, Paul teaches that God is the sovereign Creator of all that is. This means not only that God created everything but also that He rules over His creation (Psalm 103:19). Paul ends this sermon by stating the fact that God will judge everyone through His Son Jesus Christ, whom He raised from the dead.

Paul has much more to say about God's character in Acts 17, as does the rest of the Bible. In another place he summarizes the character of God in this way: "For from Him and through Him and to Him are all things. To Him be the glory forever" (Romans 11:36). This means that God is the source of all things. He is the means for all things. He is the goal of all things. He alone is worthy of glory!

God made us, knows us, is watching us at all times, and has the authority and wisdom to decree how all things should be done for His glory! There's an old-time TV show called *Father Knows Best*. While hopefully dads are knowledgeable, God, the heavenly Father, alone knows what is best every time!

Our natural tendency is to have a warped, inaccurate view of God. This often occurs in one of two ways. On the one hand, it is easy to think of God as a God of love, mercy, grace, kindness, goodness, and so on. He certainly is all these things! If this is all that normally comes to mind about God, though, you have an inaccurate view of God that will encourage you to take the demands of God more lightly than you should.

On the other hand, others only think of God as being holy, the Judge, and full of wrath. While God is all these things, He is much more than only these things! This kind of warped view tends to lead people away from God, because who wants to worship a god that is only mad at you all the time?

As a result, it is important to develop a balanced understanding of the character of God that keeps all His attributes in view at the same time. I once studied the book of Psalms to try to understand the character of God better. Every time I found a description, name, or action of God, I put it down in a list and ended up with seven pages (single-spaced) of a variety of descriptions of God that helped me to understand Him better, hopefully in a more balanced way.

An accurate view of God is essential for you to be saved from your sin and become a Christian. If you don't know who God is, you won't be able to know accurately who man is or who Jesus is, or to care enough about what God demands.

Who Man Is. It is also important to know yourself. This can be taken in a lot of different ways—your hair and eye color, your likes and dislikes, your personality, your relationships, and so on. In order to understand the gospel, though, you need to understand what the Bible says about who you are. (I am not singling you out. This is true of everyone who has ever lived and will ever live, except for Jesus Christ.)

The tricky part is that it's impossible to truly know yourself until you know God. None of what is truly important about us (such as being made in the image of God—Genesis 1:27; being sinful and in need of a Savior—Romans 5:6–10; Ephesians 2:1–10; and so on) can be understood apart from understanding God. Since God is the sovereign Creator of the universe, He alone determines what is right and wrong. Man is not free to set the rules but must follow God's rules. Knowing yourself requires that you understand what the Bible says about God.

So what does the Bible teach about who man is? Man is born dead in trespasses and sins (Ephesians 2:1). Obviously we are speaking not of literal death but of spiritual death. You may consider yourself to be very spiritual, and many people are. (This was the problem in Athens that we saw earlier in

Acts 17.) Being spiritual, however, counts only when it is based upon the truth. As a result, there will be many "spiritual" people in hell. Paul teaches that everyone is born into this world as a child of "wrath" (Ephesians 2:3) because we are sinners the very moment our life begins (Psalm 51:5). This sin nature is inherited spiritually from our parents, going all the way back to Adam (Romans 5:12).

Because we are born spiritually dead due to our sin, Paul's words in Romans 3:10–12, 23 (which quotes Psalms 14:1–3; 53:1–3) are not surprising:

> "There is none righteous, not even one;
> There is none who understands,
> There is none who seeks for God;
> All have turned aside, together they have become useless;
> There is none who does good,
> There is not even one."
>
> . . . .
>
> For all have sinned and fall short of the glory of God.

Even though it looks as if people seek God, they cannot seek the true God apart from God's creating within them the desire to do so. Even when it looks like sinners are doing good works, they are not doing them for the motives that please God, which taints everything with sin.

This sin is so profound that later, in Romans 5:6–10, Paul describes all people as helpless, ungodly, sinners, and enemies of God. Even though unforgiven sinners may show good outward behavior, their hearts are far away from God. Therefore, sinners cannot be godly. Because of sin, we are not just different from God but are actually His enemies—fighting against Him and His kingdom. But saying we are helpless means that we are without hope to deal with our own sinfulness!

This is difficult to accept when you see that little baby who smells so wonderful and makes the cutest expressions even when sneezing, yawning, and especially smiling! But, as just about any parent will say, no one had to teach that cute little baby to sin. Why is it that babies normally say the word, "No!" or "Mine!" before being able to say, "Yes"? Who teaches them to fight with their brothers and sisters and to disobey their parents? No one has to teach them these things, because they have sinful hearts already enslaved by sin.

If this were the end of the gospel story, if God left us to our own devices, there would be no hope at all in dealing with our sin! At best, all we could ever do is trade one sin for another. Thankfully, this is not all that there is to the gospel. Even though we are left helpless to rid ourselves of sin and its consequences, God is not helpless, and He has acted to save us from our sin!

Who Jesus Is. We have already looked at what Jesus did according to 1 Corinthians 15:3–7. All these elements at the core of the gospel (Jesus died, was buried, was raised, and reappeared) are essentials that must be believed. But the gospel truly makes sense only when you understand who Jesus is!

Philippians 2:6–11 looks at both the person of Jesus and the work of Jesus,

> who, although He existed in the form of God, did not regard equality with God a thing to be grasped, but emptied Himself, taking the form of a bondservant, and being made in the likeness of men. And being found in appearance as a man, He humbled Himself by becoming obedient to the point of death, even death on a cross. Therefore

also God highly exalted Him, and bestowed on Him the name which is above every name, that at the name of Jesus every knee should bow, of those who are in heaven, and on earth, and under the earth, and that every tongue should confess that Jesus Christ is Lord, to the glory of God the Father.

This passage shows that Jesus is equal with God. He is the Lord! He humbled Himself to also become a man while continuing to be God. (If this starts making your mind hurt a little bit, don't worry; you are in good company. While we see these truths clearly in God's Word, they are too great for any human to understand fully.) This humility reached its deepest depth on the cross, when He took the place of sinful people by sacrificing Himself as the substitute.

Paul describes how Jesus became our substitute in this way in 2 Corinthians 5:21: "He [God, the Father] made Him [God, the Son—Jesus] who knew no sin to be sin on our behalf, that we might become the righteousness of God in Him." Jesus, the perfect God-man, never sinned one time in any way (Hebrews 4:15). Therefore, He is qualified to pay for the sin of others. God crushed His Son (Isaiah 53:10) by taking the sin of all those who believe in Him and placing them on Jesus. In other words, Jesus was punished for our sin. God also took the righteousness of Jesus and replaced our sin with Jesus' righteousness. This is the heart of the gospel. Helpless people, who do nothing but sin, are given the righteousness of Jesus Christ in exchange for their sin. What a deal!

What God Demands. The next question, then, answers how sinful people get rid of their sin. How can we exchange our sin for Christ's righteousness? What can we do?

Answer #1—We can do absolutely nothing (John 1:12–13; Matthew 19:26). There is nothing that a helpless person can do (Romans 5:6)! If he could do something, he wouldn't be helpless.

> For by grace you have been saved through faith; and that *not of yourselves*, it is the gift of God; *not as a result of works*, that no one should boast. (Ephesians 2:8–9)

Titus 3:3–7 puts it this way:

> For we also once were foolish ourselves, disobedient, deceived, enslaved to various lusts and pleasures, spending our life in malice and envy, hateful, hating one another. But when the kindness of God our Savior and His love for mankind appeared, He saved us, *not on the basis of deeds which we have done in righteousness*, but according to His mercy, by the washing of regeneration and renewing by the Holy Spirit, whom He poured out upon us richly through Jesus Christ our Savior, that being justified by His grace we might be made heirs according to the hope of eternal life.

We are saved from our sin by God's grace (a gift that cannot be earned). Salvation comes from God, *not* from the efforts of helpless man. So the first answer to the question above is that there is nothing we can do to save ourselves from our sin.

Answer #2—We must respond with repentance and faith. As Titus 3:6 says, *God* poured this gift out upon us. All we can do is to receive this gift from God (John 1:12). But perhaps you say, "Wait a minute. Make up your mind! I thought you said we could do nothing. Now you are saying we have to do something. You are being inconsistent." I might agree with you if we had to repent and believe in our own natural strength, but the Bible is clear that the ability to repent and believe is *also* a gift of God (Romans 2:4; Ephesians 2:8–9). God demands that we obey by repenting and believing the gospel, but He enables us to obey, in the first place, by giving us the gifts of repentance and faith. So we don't do anything by ourselves; we can't. But we can receive and apply the gifts that God gives us.

The first words of Jesus in the gospel of Mark (1:15) teach us this: "The time is fulfilled, and the kingdom of God is at hand; repent and believe in the gospel." When Jesus came to the world bringing salvation for our sin, He spoke on behalf of God so that we would know how to receive the salvation He so freely offers—by repenting and believing.

These two terms are commonly misunderstood. Repentance is often accurately symbolized as a U-turn. In order to be saved from our sin, the U-turn must occur in our mind as we change our view about sin. The sin we used to love, we now hate. The sin that used to seem so satisfying, we now understand never truly satisfies.

Repentance for an unbeliever does not mean that the unbeliever has to remove all sin in order to be saved. That would require that we become perfect in order to become Christians. No one can do this. When an unbeliever repents, he changes how he thinks about sin to see it as it truly is. Then, once he is saved from his sin, this repentance is the process of changing his life to live in a way that pleases God.

The other term, "believe" (or to trust or have faith), is also a little confusing. Acts 16:31 says, "Believe in the Lord Jesus, and you shall be saved." Believing in Jesus doesn't mean that we simply believe the facts about Jesus' person and work. It certainly includes that, but, as James 2:19 puts it, "The demons also believe, and shudder." There are several accounts in the Bible when Jesus cast demons out of people. While they were being cast out, they often acknowledged the truth of who Jesus is, but they certainly did not repent (Mark 1:24, 34; 5:7). Obviously the demons believe the facts about Jesus Christ, but instead of being saved because of this belief, they shudder at the truth. It's not enough just to agree with the facts.

The gospel of John also records that people believed in Jesus but were not saved by that belief (John 2:23–25; 8:30–44). The kind of faith that saves people from their sin is not merely an academic or temporary belief of the facts.

Instead, saving faith is the kind that bears the fruit of faith—a changed lifestyle. It takes the facts of the gospel and then, by God's grace, lives according to those facts by trusting in Him. This is the focus of the book of James and more specifically James 2:14–26. Saving faith will express itself in works that show you are saved. The works themselves do not save! We've already seen that people are helpless to do anything to save themselves. But the kind of belief that results in salvation will change the way you live your life. It will cause you to do good things, because "faith without works is useless" (James 2:20) and is "dead" (James 2:26).

The faith that saves you from your sin is the faith that will encourage you to place your life in the hands of God to do with as He wants. We won't do this perfectly this side of heaven (1 John 1:8–10), but there should be progress in becoming more and more obedient to the things of God. Thankfully, God promises to finish what He has started in saving believers from their sin (Philippians 1:6). We will someday be glorified and free from all sin in the way we live (Romans 8:29–30).

If you are still uncertain about these things, I would urge you to read the gospel of John! It was written specifically "that you may believe that Jesus is the Christ, the Son of God; and that believing you may have life in His name" (John 20:31)!

Conclusion

There is no truth more important than the gospel. It is crucial, though, to get the gospel right. My prayer for all who read this book is that you will receive the gospel if you have not done so already. Then, as a true believer in Jesus Christ, you will work to glorify God in everything about your life, including modesty. The issue of modesty, therefore, is one way to measure your heart to see whether you are a child of God who delights in pleasing your Father in heaven. God's glory, His reputation, is at stake in how you, a child of God, present yourself to the world. Through His word, *He* has picked out the clothes of modesty for you to wear, the words and actions of modesty for you to live, the attitude of modesty for you to embrace, and the motive of modesty for you to glorify Him!

As you see that modesty is more than a change of clothes, you will someday get to hear different words from Jesus on that judgment day than those terrifying words we saw at the beginning of this chapter. It might sound something like this: "Well done, good and faithful slave. . . . Enter into the joy of your master" (Matthew 25:21, 23)!

Review Questions

1. What verses could be the scariest words that the Lord Jesus spoke? In these verses, He was talking about people who *think* they are Christians but are not.
2. Read the entire book of 1 John (it is not very long). List all the verses that tell you how you can be sure that you are a Christian.
3. According to 1 Corinthians 15:1–8, what is the gospel?

4. Match the following:

Jesus told His disciples that He would die.	Romans 4:25
Jesus rose from the dead.	Mark 10:33-34
Paul told the Jews about the resurrected Jesus appearing to him.	Acts 22:3-21
The resurrection is the reason for our salvation.	Matthew 28:1-6

5. Read John 14:6 and Acts 4:12. Could there be salvation any other way than through the Lord Jesus?
6. Match the following:

God is the source of all things.	Philippians 2:6-11
Man is born a sinner.	2 Corinthians 5:21
Our sin natures were inherited from Adam.	Romans 5:12
In spite of our sin, Christ died for us.	Romans 5:6-10
Jesus is equal with God. He is Lord.	Ephesians 2:1
Jesus was punished for our sin.	Romans 11:36

7. Read Titus 3:3–7. How many good deeds do you have to do to earn God's favor?
8. See John 20:31. Why did the apostle John write the gospel of John?
9. What is your prayer?

APPENDIX

A Letter to Parents

Dear Parents,

We want to appeal to you as fellow parents. We will stand before God and give account for our families. Our parental goal regarding modesty is to work to instill it at a heart level. It isn't enough just to exchange immodest clothes for modest ones. Modesty must be owned by the heart, since modesty is more than just a change of clothes. By God's grace, parents need to encourage in their children a desire for modesty, springing from a love for God, that will withstand the pull of an immodest culture.

You have a responsibility to encourage your daughter to honor God by speaking and acting modestly in her interaction with guys and by dressing modestly to cover what God wants covered. Hopefully you are already working faithfully at this. Even if you are uncomfortable or even feel like a hypocrite, you must not abandon your responsibility in this matter.

Know what is in your daughter's closet. As she grows and matures as a young woman, make sure that the modest outfit of yesterday is still modest today. Modesty requires constant vigilance. It is easiest to start the process of instilling modesty early, preferably before puberty transforms your little girl. If you have missed this opportunity, you must still help your daughter to understand what is at stake in this crucial area.

It is helpful to go shopping with your daughter in order to understand the battle of finding modest clothing that honors God and pleases your daughter. You get the side benefit of spending extra time with her. It might also explain why she always wants more money for clothes! Another good reason is that you might find it easier to understand the frustration that comes with try-ing to find the precious few pieces of modest clothing that your daughter will find acceptable.

It is not wise to control every clothing choice your daugh-ter makes! Your responsibility is to make sure that she is not violating the commands of God. When she is within the moral bounds of God's will—when she is dressing modestly—then it is wise to allow her to express her own preferences according to her own tastes. If she is dressing modestly but you don't like her choices, this may not be the hill for you to die on. There are typically enough issues that parents need to address without mandating their own preferences. Our goal as parents is to raise godly children, not to make clones of ourselves or seek in them the fulfillment of our dreams.

While these are challenging issues, they are worth pursuing! Thankfully, you are not on your own in this if you are a Christian. These are God's concerns, and He will help you as you follow His will. He has also given you a church body as a help.

Your faithfulness in this area has eternal benefits. The faith-ful servant of God may hear these words when he stands before God on judgment day:

> Well done, good and faithful slave; you were faithful with a few things, I will put you in charge of many things; enter into the joy of your master. (Matthew 25:23)

May God bless your faithfulness in this area!

—MARTHA PEACE AND KENT KELLER

Notes

Chapter 1: What Is Immodesty, Anyway?

1. When the Bible refers to the "heart," it never refers to the physical organ that pumps the blood around in one's body. Neither לֵב (leb) in the Old Testament nor καρδία (kardia) in the New Testament ever refers to the physical organ.

Chapter 2: How Are Guys So Different?

1. Karen Lee-Thorp and Cynthia Hicks, *Why Beauty Matters* (Colorado Springs: Navpress, 1997), 108.
2. Shaunti Feldhahn, *For Women Only* (Sisters, OR: Multnomah Publishers, 2004), 133–34.
3. Richard Baxter, "A Christian Directory," *Baxter's Practical Works*, vol. 1 (London: George Virtue; repr., Ligonier, PA: Soli Deo Gloria, 1990), 392.

Part Two: The Old Testament on Immodesty

1. This statement in 2 Timothy 3:16 also includes the New Testament. In 1 Timothy 5:18, Paul considers Jesus' words, found in Luke 10:7, to be Scripture.

Chapter 3: Why Should I Wear Clothes?

1. Support for the fact that sin is what brought shame to Adam and Eve is found in the broader context of Genesis 2–3 (see especially 2:25; 3:7, 10). Shame often accompanies sinful nakedness—see Genesis 9:22–23; Exodus 20:26; 28:42–43; Leviticus 18:6, 10; 20:17–19; 1 Samuel 20:30; 2 Samuel 10:1–5; Job 8:22; Isaiah 20:4; Ezekiel 16:37; Hosea 2:3, 9; Micah 1:11; Nahum 3:5; Revelation 3:18. The following passages show that sometimes God even punished sin by making people naked to shame them for

their sin—Isaiah 47:8; Jeremiah 4:30; Ezekiel 16:35–43; 33:31–32; Nahum 3:1–7; 2 Corinthians 5:2–4; Revelation 16:15.

2. William Gesenius, *The New Brown, Driver, and Briggs Hebrew and English Lexicon of the Old Testament*, trans. Edward Robinson, ed. France Brown with the cooperation of S. R. Driver and Charles A. Briggs (1907; repr., Boston: Houghton Mifflin, 1981), 292 (hereafter cited as BDB).

3. Edwin Yamauchi, *Theological Wordbook of the Old Testament*, vol. 1, eds. R. Laird Harris, Gleason L. Archer Jr., and Bruce K. Waltke (Chicago: Moody, 1980), 605.

4. Ibid.

5. Derek Kidner, *Genesis* (Downer's Grove, IL: IVP, 1967), 69.

6. BDB, 509.

Chapter 4: Why Were Women Immodest in the Old Testament?

1. James Bruckner, *Jonah, Nahum, Habakkuk, Zephaniah*, The NIV Application Commentary (Grand Rapids: Zondervan, 2004), 288.

Chapter 5: Who Are Immodesty's Best Friends in the Old Testament?

1. See also 1 Corinthians 16:20; 2 Corinthians 13:12; 1 Thessalonians 5:26; 1 Peter 5:14).

2. See Mark 7:22; Romans 13:13; 2 Corinthians 12:21; Galatians 5:19; Ephesians 4:19; 1 Timothy 5:11; 1 Peter 4:3; 2 Peter 2:2, 7–18; Revelation 18:3, 7, 9. The Greek words for "sensuality" (ασελγεια [*aselgeia*], καταστρηνιαω [*katastreniao*], στρηνιαω [*streniao*], στρηνος [*strenos*]) are often translated as "sensual," "lustful," or "licentious" (living outside the boundaries of the law).

3. See Isaiah 47:8; Jeremiah 4:30; Ezekiel 33:31–32.

4. This passage has seven references to sensuality—Ezekiel 23:5, 7, 9, 11, 12, 16, 20.

5. These women symbolize Samaria and Jerusalem. The men of royalty for whom they have a sensual desire symbolize Egypt, Assyria, and Babylon. In this metaphor, Israel is "married" to

God, but commits "adultery" by forming treaties with these countries and pursuing them rather than depending upon God.

6. See also Genesis 2:25; Proverbs 5:15–21; and 1 Corinthians 7:2–5.

7. See also Job 8:22; Psalms 35:26; 109:29; 132:18. The New Testament also reveals this close relationship between nakedness and shame in Revelation 3:18; 16:15.

8. עֵרוָה ('ervah), BDB, 788–89. See also Isaiah 20:4; Lamentations 1:8; Ezekiel 16:22, 37, 39; 22:10; Micah 1:11—even though these passages apply this concept metaphorically to the vulnerability of a city's defenses.

9. Another example of this is found in 1 Samuel 19:24. Most scholars believe that Saul was not completely naked but had merely removed his outer garments while leaving on undergarments.

10. See Proverbs 2:16–19; 5:1–14, 20–23; 6:20–35; 7:6–27; 9:13–18.

11. See Leviticus 18:6–20; 20:17–21; 1 Samuel 20:30; Lamentations 1:8; Ezekiel 16:37; 23:10, 29 (Walter C. Kaiser Jr., *Toward Old Testament Ethics* [Grand Rapids: Zondervan, 1983], 192).

12. See Leviticus 18:6–20; 20:11, 17–21; Deuteronomy 22:30; 24:1; 27:20.

13. Kate Betts, "Looks like a Cover-up," *Time*, March 13, 2006, 60.

Part Three: The New Testament on Immodesty

1. See "The Role of Women," *Grace to You*, 2002, http://www.gty.org/resources/distinctives/dd08/the-role-of-women. See also James A. Borland, "Women in the Life and Teachings of Jesus," in *Recovering Biblical Manhood and Womanhood*, eds. John Piper and Wayne Grudem (Wheaton, IL: Crossway, 1991), 113–20; and James B. Hurley, *Man and Woman in Biblical Perspective* (Leicester, England: IVP, 1981), 82–112.

2. Karen Lee-Thorp and Cynthia Hicks, *Why Beauty Matters* (Colorado Springs: Navpress, 1997), 147.

Chapter 6: Why Were Women Immodest in the New Testament?

1. I learned this phrase from Dr. George Zemek, my seminary theology professor, who uses it in reference to Hebrews 4:12.

Chapter 7: What's Wrong with Being Immodest?

1. "Having dealt with the disruptive men, Paul turns to the disruptive women" (William D. Mounce, *Pastoral Epistles*, Word Biblical Commentary 46, ed. Bruce M. Metzger [Nashville: Thomas Nelson Publishers, 2000], 108). "Paul turns next to women (without the definite article, implying a broader context than merely wives)" (Gordon D. Fee, *1 & 2 Timothy, Titus*, New International Biblical Commentary [Peabody, MA: Hendrickson, 1988], 71). "Just as Paul was asking not only husbands but men in general to pray, so also he is enjoining women in general, not just wives, to dress modestly and discreetly, and to behave in accord with their womanliness in relation to men" (George William Knight III, *The Pastoral Epistles*, The New International Greek Testament Commentary [Grand Rapids: Eerdmans, 1992], 133).

2. Melody Green, *Uncovering the Truth about Modesty* (Lindale, TX: Last Days Ministries, 1982), available online at http://www.lastdaysministries.org/Articles/1000008635/Last_Days_Ministries/LDM/Discipleship_Teachings/Melody_Green/Uncovering_The_Truth.aspx. Emphasis original.

3. Donald Guthrie, *The Pastoral Epistles*, Tyndale New Testament Commentaries, ed. R. V. G. Tasker (Grand Rapids: Eerdmans, 1983), 74.

4. Walter Bauer, *A Greek-English Lexicon of the New Testament and Other Early Christian Literature*, 2nd ed., revised and augmented by F. W. Gingrich and Frederick Danker (Chicago: The University of Chicago Press, 1979), 445; G. Abbott-Smith, *A Manual Greek Lexicon of the New Testament* (Edinburgh: T&T Clark, 1986), 254; John Henry Thayer, *A Greek-English Lexicon of the New Testament* (Wheaton, IL: Evangel Publishing Company, 1974), 356.

5. John MacArthur Jr., *1 Timothy*, The MacArthur New Testament Commentary (Chicago: Moody Bible Institute, 1995), 79.

6. καταστολη (*katastole*) (Mounce, *Pastoral Epistles*, 109; Bauer, *A Greek-English Lexicon*, 419).

7. Mounce, *Pastoral Epistles*, 109.

8. Don De Welt, *Paul's Letters to Timothy and Titus* (Joplin, MO: College Press, 1961), 54.

9. MacArthur, *1 Timothy*, 81.

10. Ibid. 81–82.

11. Gaius Plinius Secundus (Pliny the Elder), *Natural History*, 9:117.

Chapter 8: Am I Free to Choose What I Want to Wear?

1. I do not remember when I first came across this acronym, but this concept did not originate with me.

Chapter 9: How Can I Avoid Legalism in Modesty?

1. "Filthy rags" are literally soiled menstrual cloths (BDB, 723).

2. This concept comes from Todd Murray, "Grace Alone" (sermon, Grace Bible Church, Brandon, FL, October 29, 2005).

Chapter 10: So, How Can I Be Modest?

1. Haley DiMarco, *Sexy Girls* (Grand Rapids: Revell, 2006), 72.

2. Carolyn Mahaney and Nicole Mahaney Whitacre, *Girl Talk* (Wheaton, IL: Crossway, 2005), 205–8.

3. Carolyn Mahaney, Nicole Whitacre, Kristin Chesemore, and Janelle Bradshaw, "Modesty Heart Check," Sovereign Grace Ministries, accessed May 14, 2015, http://www.sovereign gracestore.com/Product/A1170-06-59/Modesty_Heart_Check _-_Checklist.aspx. The download is currently available free of charge.

4. Shannon Ethridge and Stephen Arterburn, *Every Young Woman's Battle* (Colorado Springs: Waterbrook Press, 2004), 94–96.

5. Jeff Pollard, *Christian Modesty and the Public Undressing of America* (Pensacola, FL: Mt. Zion Publications), 1999.

6. Melody Green, *Uncovering the Truth about Modesty* (Lindale, TX: Last Days Ministries, 1982), available online at http://www .lastdaysministries.org/Articles/1000008635/Last_Days _Ministries/LDM/Discipleship_Teachings/Melody_Green /Uncovering_The_Truth.aspx. Emphasis original.

7. "Are Christian Women 'Modeling Modesty' in Weddings?," The Albert Mohler Radio Program, May 16, 2006, available online at http://www.albertmohler.com/2006/05/16/are-christian -women-modeling-modesty-in-weddings/.

8. This list is a summary of the main points of John Barnett, "Clothe Yourselves with Christ" (sermon, August 22, 2004), available online at Discover the Book Ministries, http://www .dtbm.org/sermon/clothe-yourselves-with-christ/.

Chapter 11: What Should I Do about This?

1. "Jessica's Plea," *Who Framed Roger Rabbit*, directed by Robert Zemeckis (1988; Burbank, CA: Buena Vista Home Entertainment, 2003), DVD.

2. C. J. Mahaney, *Humility*, (Sisters, OR: Multnomah Publishers, 2005), 65–66.

Chapter 12: What Hope Is There for the Immodest?

1. As a noun—Matthew 4:23; 9:35; 24:14; 26:13; Mark 1:1, 14, 15; 8:35; 10:29; 13:10; 14:9; Acts 15:7; 20:24; 21:8; Romans 1:1, 9, 16; 2:16; 10:16; 11:28; 15:16, 19; 16:25; 1 Corinthians 4:15; 9:12, 14 (two times), 18 (two times), 23; 15:1; 2 Corinthians 2:12; 4:3, 4; 8:18; 9:13; 10:14; 11:4, 7; Galatians 1:6, 7, 11; 2:2, 5, 7, 14; Ephesians 1:13; 3:6; 4:11; 6:15, 19; Philippians 1:5, 7, 12, 16, 27 (two times); 2:22; 4:3, 15; Colossians 1:5, 23; 1 Thessalonians 1:5; 2:2, 4, 8, 9; 3:2; 2 Thessalonians 1:8; 2:14; 1 Timothy 1:11; 2 Timothy 1:8, 10; 2:8; 4:5; Philemon 1:13; 1 Peter 4:17; Revelation 14:6.

   As a verb—Matthew 11:5; Luke 1:19; 2:10; 4:18, 43; 7:22; 8:1; 9:6; 16:16; 20:1; Acts 5:42; 8:4, 12; 10:36; 11:20; 13:32; 14:7, 15, 21; 15:35; 16:10; Romans 1:15; 10:15; 15:20; 1 Corinthians 1:17; 9:16

(two times), 18; 2 Corinthians 10:16; Galatians 1:8, 9, 11, 16, 23; Ephesians 3:8; 1 Thessalonians 3:6; Hebrews 4:6; 1 Peter 1:12, 25; Revelation 14:6.

2. This outline is borrowed from a great book to read for a more thorough treatment of the gospel: J. I. Packer, *Evangelism and the Sovereignty of God* (Downer's Grove, IL: InterVarsity Press, 1961).

Index of Scripture